Heavenly REWARDS

SIMMS S. MULOZI

Foreword By Pukuta Mwanz

CONTENTS

DEDICATION

This book is dedicated to every believer, *"...to make ready a people prepared for the Lord"* (Luke 1:17b). Your service to the Lord is not in vain.

My heart particularly goes out to the believers around the world who are facing great persecution for the word of God and the testimony of Jesus. May this book be a source of comfort in your suffering for Christ Jesus our Lord. May the hope of His return fill you with joy as you labour for Him

Then finally, I owe it to the future generations who will be the torch-bearers of the eternal and glorious gospel of our Lord Jesus Christ. Run your race and finish your course for the time of His return is upon us!

ACKNOWLEDGMENTS

I would never have been able to write this book without the grace of our Lord Jesus Christ Who deserves full credit for it.

To my father, Mr Samuel L. Mulozi, your polished communication skills have impacted my own. I am indeed grateful for your support and the values I have inherited from you.

I deeply appreciate the moral support of my brothers and sisters who are my greatest fans.

I wish to salute the men who have been my spiritual role models. These are Pastors Walker Schurz, William Kantumoya, Gabriel Schultz, and David A. Newberry. Thank you for watching over my soul as good shepherds under the Good Shepherd.

Reverend Pukuta Mwanza, your editorial input and sound advice after examining the content of this book has helped to better refine it. I also thank you so much for writing the foreword.

It is also my pleasure to acknowledge and thank Mwitumwa "MT" Kanyanga and Sitwala Mulozi my brother for lending me their laptop and desktop respectively to type out the handwritten notes that evolved into this book.

Chilufya Mulundu, you are appreciated for not only printing the first draft for me to read, but for helping to proof-read as well as provide constructive criticism. You believed and showed excitement for this project as though it were your own.

To Luo Punabantu Zacks, thank you for your excellent job in copy-editing.

Last, but not least, I would also like to acknowledge the authors whose writings have greatly enriched my understanding of the subject matter. These include Dr Hilton Sutton, Charles Capps, Finis Dake, Jimmy Swaggart, Gordon Lindsay, Salem Kirban, Chuck Swindol and Rick Joyner.

FOREWORD

The rapture is one of the most profound events in the world which will soon take place and will lead to a global disaster of enormous magnitude unlike any catastrophe ever experienced in human history. It will be a disaster on the one hand because the sudden disappearance of millions of believers from the face of the earth will lead to machines, motor vehicles, planes, control rooms, hospital theatre rooms, railway systems, ships and all sorts of high speed machinery to suddenly be in disarray and out of control when within the twinkling of an eye believers in charge of all those operations will be instantaneously raptured. This event will be so sudden and unpredictable that it can even happen just before you finish reading this foreword. On the other hand, this event is a glorious expectation of every born again believer. It will be an event that will usher in the close of the age leading to the eternal destiny of mankind.

Our earthly journey is connected to our mission for the Lord. Believers' service will be rewarded by the Lord in proportion to what they have achieved for His Kingdom. While eternal life is a free gift being given to believers by the grace of God, rewards will be given based on performance - how one has lived his or her Christian life. Just as there are rewards here on earth for people that successfully undertake and complete their tasks, or competitions, there will be rewards given in heaven to the faithful servants of our Lord. This book provides a unique approach to understanding the events that precede the awards in heaven. It also explains in great detail and chronological order a series of very important biblical events that will take place before the eternal perfect state.

Believers should live their lives with dedication and faithfulness to God. On the last day, the Lord Jesus Christ will receive the faithful servants and welcome them into his Kingdom. Our little time of service here on earth will be compensated with heavenly rewards that are eternal and incorruptible. Many people on earth strive for temporal things that do not have much value or sustainable use. The work we do for the Lord will not go unnoticed regardless of whether or not such work seems insignificant to us. Every deed will be accounted for and God will give each one of us a 'just' recompense of reward in proportion to our faithfulness in service to Him. Simms' passion for the 'Heavenly Rewards' will inspire you to start developing a spiritual mind-set and commitment towards the heavenly calling. The time for receiving heavenly rewards will be preceded by the rapture. This is a mystery because there is no human ingenuity that can predict with highest levels of accuracy and precision when that event will take place. Therefore, the only way to get ready is primarily to be born again and then to live the rest of our lives in the light of the fact that this event can take place anytime. Therefore, we should be living each moment for the Lord.

Pukuta N. Mwanza B.Min.Sc., MA(RSD), MA(Org.L) (Rev.)

Executive Director

Evangelical Fellowship of Zambia

INTRODUCTION: Prepare For Eternity

There are many prizes or awards that people aspire for in this world. The Olympic Gold Medal, World Cup, and Super Bowl are among the most prestigious prizes in the world of sport. The Grammys and the Oscars grace those with the most outstanding skill in the music and film industries.

It is indeed a joy to be crowned Footballer of the Year, Most Outstanding Student of the Year, Employee of the Month, Businesswoman of the Year or even Miss World. The monetary benefits that accompany winning the Nobel Peace Prize alone can improve one's economic and social life to a very large degree.

This system of rewarding and awarding people for their efforts has motivated many to perform far better than they otherwise would. The prospect of winning a prize has kept many an athlete training and competing consistently in spite of aching muscles and mental or physical fatigue. They paid the necessary price to win the prize.

By the same token, God has an even better reward system of which the earthly system is but a shadow. His rewards are too glorious to be compared with any earthly prize. The heavenly crowns, thrones, robes, and kingly rulership that they represent are far beyond what you or I could ever imagine. Yet God has been gracious enough to let us know about how to win them because He wants the very best of eternity for us.

Soon and very soon the heavenly trumpet will sound and the Lord will call up to Him those who are spiritually ready to go with Him to heaven for the greatest of all prize-giving days. Can you hear the majestic voice of Jesus saying, "Behold, I am coming soon! My reward is with me, and I will give to everyone according to what he has done?" (Revelation 22:12)

Indeed a day of reckoning is coming when we shall give an account to God for our earthly life. Knowing there's an examination ahead should motivate us to prepare adequately. During that examination we will be graded according to our works – the quality of our life here on earth. We determine what we will get. It is therefore important to understand what is required of us to receive a worthy mark on that day. *"For we must all appear before the Judgment Seat of Christ; that everyone may receive the things done in his body, according to that he hath done, whether it be good or bad"* (2 Corinthians 5:10 KJV).

But while the spiritually prepared Christians will be in heaven receiving their rewards, the remaining inhabitants of the earth will be experiencing a time of great tribulation unequalled since man first appeared on the earth. This is when an evil world ruler known as the Antichrist will be revealed.

However, the good news is that at the end of the Antichrist's seven-year rule, Jesus and all the believers in heaven will return to the earth, defeat the Antichrist and his armies and set up the glorious millennial Kingdom of Christ. Then once the one thousand year reign is over, the resurrection of all the wicked dead for judgment will take place. Finally the devil and all the wicked people of every generation will forever be banished from God's holy presence never to be remembered again. They will experience never-ending punishment in the lake of fire.

Immediately after this, the Lord will create a new atmospheric heaven (sky) and recreate this earth into a brand new global paradise. God's grand plan, His original, ultimate and eternal dream for mankind will at last be realized in all its fullness. God will finally dwell with His children and the angels in uninterrupted bliss throughout the endless ages of eternity. "He will wipe every tear from their eyes, and there will be no more death or sorrow or crying or pain. All these things are gone forever." (Revelation 21:4 NLT)

This book you are holding is a revelation of the roadmap to that most glorious destination. Read it prayerfully and meditatively. It could mean the difference between a full reward or no reward. Make no mistake about it: the quality of your preparation determines your level of performance. Everything you do today is of eternal consequence. I pray that everyone who reads this book will live their lives in such a way as not to suffer loss at the Judgment Seat of Christ but to obtain a full reward and enjoy a most blissful eternity.

May you hear Him say:

> *"Well done, good and faithful servant; thou hast been faithful over a few things, I will make thee ruler over many things: enter thou into the joy of thy lord"* (Matthew 25:23 KJV).

CHAPTER 1

THE RAPTURE OF THE CHURCH

One of the greatest promises Jesus made to us is in John 14:2-3. This is what He said:

> *"In my Father's house are many rooms; if it were not so, I would have told you. I am going there to prepare a place for you. And if I go and prepare a place for you, I will come back and take you to be with me that you also may be where I am."*

Jesus is coming back to take His own people out of this world to heaven before the world undergoes a time of tribulation unequalled from the beginning of time. This event where Jesus comes in the air and calls His people to ascend to where He is waiting for them is popularly referred to as the rapture. To be more specific, it is the rapture of the church.

However, the word rapture itself is not found in the bible. It is a word originating from Latin that carries with it the meaning of great joy and of something great happening suddenly. The rapture of the church then is the sudden catching away of the church by Jesus from earth to Himself. At Jesus' command, suddenly all over the world, the bodies of godly people who had died will come out of graves and other places and will ascend to be reunited with the spirits of their owners who have descended with Christ in the air. These will be immortal bodies that will forever shine with God's glory. Then immediately after this the godly people who are alive on earth will be transformed and also ascend to where Jesus is awaiting them in the air just before proceeding to heaven to reward them for their faithful service on earth.

Please note that this is not the time when Jesus will appear to the whole world and set up His one thousand year rule on earth.

The rapture is only an appearance for believers whereas His return at the battle of Armageddon is an appearance to the whole world. A period of seven years separates the two appearances which are actually two phases of His second coming. So first He's coming *for* the saints and second He's coming *with* the saints. In the rapture He doesn't land on earth but meets the saints in the air. In His glorious appearing to the whole world, He lands with the saints on earth, defeats the antichrist at Armageddon and establishes His millennial reign. What separates the two appearances is the seven year tribulation period.

The rapture of the church will indeed shake this world to its core. There is no telling how panic-stricken those left behind will be. But how glorious an experience it will be for those who have been awaiting His return! 1 Thessalonians 4:14-18 paints a vivid picture of that dramatic event.

> *"We believe that Jesus died and rose again and so we believe that God will bring with Jesus those who have fallen asleep in Him. According to the Lord's own word, we tell you that we who are still alive, who are left till the coming of the Lord, will certainly not precede those who have fallen asleep. For the Lord Himself will come down from heaven, with a loud command, with the voice of the archangel and with the trumpet call of God, and the dead in Christ will rise first. After that, we who are still alive and are left will be caught up together with them in the clouds to meet the Lord in the air. And so we will be with the Lord forever. Therefore encourage each other with these words."*

Now here's a side thought. Do you suppose the rapture will be silent or loud? Is Jesus just going to sneak us out of this world? Or is the world going to hear that trumpet blast? It is not so clear but according to the passage you've just read this event seems to be a very noisy, earth shaking event. The Lord's shout, the archangel's voice and the trumpet call of God are certainly not silent. The voice of the Lord alone is like the thunderous sound of many waters. Draw your own conclusion.

Three Views on the Rapture

There are three views on the rapture. These views are as follows:

- **Pre-tribulation rapture** – This view is held by those who believe that the rapture will take place just before the tribulation begins. This implies that the rapture will signal the beginning of the seven-year tribulation.
- **Mid-tribulation rapture** – Those who hold this view are convinced that the rapture of the church takes place half-way through the seven-year tribulation period.
- **Post-tribulation** – Those holding this view say that the church will go through the tribulation and be raptured at the end. They are convinced that the church will be tested, tried and consequently purified by going through the tribulation.

Personally after studying the subject for a while now I have found that the other events of bible prophecy fit so much better with the pre-tribulation view of the rapture. This is the view I hold and I think Revelation 3:10 is a promise from Jesus that the church does not have to go through any part of the tribulation: *"Since you have kept my command to endure patiently, I will also keep you from **the hour of trial** that is going to come upon the **whole world** to test those who live on the earth."*

But regardless of whether you are Pri-Trib, Mid-Trib or Post-Trib, the fact remains the same. There is a rapture of the church and you must be ready for it! One preacher puts it humorously. He says he is Pan-Trib. He believes it will all pan-out in the end! Anyway, it's not about who is right and who is wrong. It's about who is ready! Your readiness for the rapture is more important than your doctrinal view of when it occurs. Readiness for His coming is what Jesus Himself emphasized. In teaching His disciples about His coming using the Parable of the Ten Virgins He said, *"But while they were on their way to buy the oil, the bridegroom arrived. The virgins who were ready went in with him to the wedding banquet. And the door was shut."* Matthew 25:10

The Day the Rapture Happens

There have been books and articles written by people who have tried to predict the year or date of the rapture. Some have even made their predictions while preaching to people. But one thing is for sure: there is no verse of scripture that tells us when the rapture will take place. That is why when the apostles asked the resurrected Christ about the time He would restore the kingdom to Israel, *"He said to them: It is not for you to know the times or dates the Father has set by His own authority."* Acts 1:7 I can't say it any better than Jesus. There is no body who knows the date of the rapture. Anybody claiming they know is deceived.

Several Raptures

You may be surprised to discover that there are several raptures found in the bible. These are accounts where people are transported to heaven in bodily form without seeing death or after being resurrected.

1. Enoch

The first person to ever be raptured in the bible is Enoch. He was a man who walked in such intimacy with God that his body became immortalized. He stepped out of time into eternity with God. Hebrews 11:5 says,

> *"By faith Enoch was taken from this life, so that he did not experience death; he could not be found, because God had taken him away. For before he was taken, he was commended as one who pleased God."*

It is clear that faith had something to do with Enoch's rapture. Could it be any different for us since Jesus said, *"...However, when the Son of man comes will He find faith on the earth?"* (Luke 18:8).

2. Elijah

The second person to go to heaven without dying is Elijah. His dramatic account is recorded for us in 2 Kings 2:1, 11:

> *"When the Lord was about to take Elijah up to heaven in a whirlwind, Elijah and Elisha were on their way from Gilgal...As they were walking along and talking together, suddenly a chariot of fire appeared and separated the two of them, and Elijah went up to heaven in a whirlwind."*

Elijah was supernaturally translated from this life to heaven. He was taken up to heaven by the Spirit of God. His experience gives us hope that we too can expect to be translated when Jesus comes to take the saints who are prepared to go to heaven with Him. Elijah knew that he was going because God told him. He stayed in tune with the Spirit just like we are supposed to if we are to hear Him say, *"Come up here"* (Revelation 4:1).

3. Jesus

Jesus is the third example of someone who was translated from earth to heaven in bodily form. Luke 24:51 says, *"While he was blessing them, he left them and was taken up into heaven."*

Jesus' rapture is the most significant. He slowly ascended to heaven as the disciples looked on. Acts 1:9-11 gives us a little more detail:

"After He said this, He was taken up before their very eyes, and a cloud hid Him from their sight. They were looking intently up into the sky as He was going, when suddenly two men dressed in white stood beside them. 'Men of Galilee,' they said, 'why do you stand here looking into the sky? This same Jesus, who has been taken from you into heaven, will come back in the same way you have seen Him go into Heaven.'"

4. The Church

The Church is not a particular denomination but rather a company of believers who are serving Jesus Christ in anticipation of His return. They are like the five wise virgins of Matthew 25 waiting for their bridegroom to arrive. They are walking in the Spirit and living by faith, ready to go at a moment's notice.

So the rapture of the Church is not the rapture of just one person but of a great company of believers who are looking forward to His return. It could be millions or possibly billions of souls. When the saints are raptured they will go to appear before the Judgment Seat of Christ to give an account for their lives. Some will be rewarded some will not.

5. The 144,000 Jews

The 144,000 Jews spoken of in the 14th chapter of Revelation is a company of Jewish believers who have an assignment to win the lost during the tribulation. There is no doubt that many souls will turn to Christ as a result of their evangelistic effort. It is clear from the following passage that Jesus comes down to meet the 144,000 Jews on Mount Zion and takes them up to heaven:

"Then I looked, and there before me was the Lamb, standing on Mount Zion, and with Him 144,000 who had His name and His Father's name written on their foreheads...And they sang a new song before the throne and before the four living creatures and the elders. No

one could learn the song except the 144,000 who had been redeemed from the earth" (Revelation 14:1, 3).

In verse one they are on the earth with Jesus. But from verse two onwards they are in heaven. Verse three tells us exactly how they got there. They *"...had been redeemed from the earth."* They don't die but are taken by Jesus up into heaven. While they are on earth, not even the Antichrist is allowed to harm them. They are supernaturally protected by God until Jesus takes them to heaven alive. They experience their own special rapture.

It has been said by some that these 144,000 Jews are the only ones going to heaven while every other godly person will only inherit the earth. The whole truth of the matter is that both heaven and earth make up our eternal home. It can't be put more clearly than what 2 Peter 3:13 says: *"But in keeping with His promise we are looking forward to a new heaven and a new earth, the home of righteousness."* The Bible also assures us that where Christ is right now in heaven, there we will be also at His coming (John 14:2-3). Then again if the 144,000 are the only ones to go to Heaven then why did John see a countless multitude of all kinds of people standing before God's throne in heaven? *"After this I looked and there before me was a great multitude that no-one could count, from every nation, tribe, people and language, standing before the throne and in front of the Lamb. They were wearing white robes and were holding palm branches in their hands."* (Revelation 7:9)

6. The Two Witnesses

The two witnesses mentioned in Revelation 11 are God's specially chosen representatives whose identity has not been made known to us. Some have supposed they are Enoch and Elijah because they never experienced death, while others say it is Moses and Elijah since they appeared to Jesus on the Mount of Transfiguration. The Bible, however, does not reveal their identity. It is, therefore, best to be silent where the Bible is silent and speak boldly where the Bible is clear. However, these two unnamed witnesses have a special assignment to prophesy to

18

the world during the great tribulation. After their assignment is over, the Lord will allow the Antichrist to kill them. But this is only so that God can demonstrate His mighty power to the whole world by resurrecting the witnesses after three and a half days. You can read Revelation 11:1-14 to get the full account but let's zero in on verses 11 and 12:

> *"But after the three and a half days, a breath of life from God entered them, and they stood on their feet, and terror struck those who saw them. They heard a loud voice from heaven saying to them, "Come up here". And they went up to heaven in a cloud, while their enemies looked on."*

This clearly shows us that they also get to experience their own rapture at the end of the tribulation.

Are You Going In The Rapture?

Now let's take a closer look at the rapture of the Church. This is the one that concerns us the most. The rapture of the Church is a subject of great importance for everyone of us. None of us wants to be left behind when Jesus comes to take away the saints – the believers – from this earth. The word of God has much to say on the subject and it will profit us to learn what the Bible says.

Let's begin with the following verse of Scripture:

> *"Listen, I tell you a mystery: we will not all sleep, but we will all be changed – in a flash, in the twinkling of an eye, at the last trumpet. For the trumpet will sound, the dead will be raised imperishable, and we will be changed"* (1 Corinthians 15:51-52).

Here the Apostle Paul tells us that we will not all die, but there will be those who will be alive when Jesus comes to take away the Church. The dead in Christ will be raised, never to die again. The bodies of those who are alive and those who are resurrected will become immortal. They will be like the glorified body of Jesus – not subject to death, disease or natural limitation. These glorified bodies – like the body of Jesus – will be able to pass through walls, disappear from one place and appear in another, and yes we'll be able to even fly. We'll have supernatural powers if you will. Our bodies will so shine with God's glory that the bible says an individual glorified body will shine like the sun. Then what do you suppose the light will be like when we all shine together? This is our glory, this is our hope.

Jesus clearly talked about the rapture when He said,

> *"In my Father's house are many rooms; if it were not so, I would have told you. I am going there to prepare a place for you. And if I go and prepare a place for you, **I will come back and take you to be with me** that you also may be where I am"* (John 14:2-3).

This is one of the greatest promises to ever come from the lips of Jesus. Indeed the Bible calls it our blessed hope.

It amazes me how many of God's people are ignorant of this very important event. If they knew, surely they would live their lives differently. It is important that we know, and like I said in the introduction, it could mean the difference between a full reward and no reward (even though some may get a partial reward). The teaching about the coming of Jesus is to prepare us for His return.

I don't know about you, but looking forward to the coming of the Lord helps me make adjustments in my life. It helps me see my life from an eternal perspective. I want to live holy because of it. I want to pray more, lead the lost to Jesus and fulfill God's plan for my life. It inspires me and motivates me to live my life for Him. I pray that everyone who reads this book will be prepared to meet the Lord at His coming. I don't even want to think of anybody remaining behind. We must learn what it takes to be prepared if we are to qualify to go in the rapture. If you are a backslidden Christian you had better get back to Jesus quick! And if you've never asked Jesus to be the Lord of your life then you had better repent right now. So whether you are backslidden or not a Christian, pray this prayer:

> **Dear Heavenly Father, I repent of my sins to follow you. I believe that Jesus died, was buried and was raised to life again for my salvation. I now receive Him in my heart and confess that Jesus is the Lord of my life. I also ask for grace to fulfill your purpose and to be ready to meet Christ at His coming. I thank You Father in Jesus' name.**

Will Babies and Little Children Be Left Behind?

Many have wondered whether or not babies and little children will go in the rapture. Will they remain behind to face the great tribulation? Well, I believe Jesus Himself answered that question in Matthew 19:14 (AMP):

> *"But He said, 'Leave the children alone! Allow the little ones to come to Me, and do not forbid or restrain or hinder them, for of such [as these] is the kingdom of heaven composed.'"*

The Lord is far more interested in babies and little children than we realize. Babies and little children who have not reached the age where they can be held accountable for their actions will most definitely be taken up to heaven when the trumpet sounds. Hundreds of millions of babies will disappear from the face of the earth. Imagine how many nursery schools will instantaneously have empty classrooms with the teachers wondering where the kids have disappeared to. How many doctors and parents will greatly panic when the labor ward is suddenly emptied of all the babies? Even the mortuary attendant will be bewildered to discover that every dead baby's body has gone missing not to mention some adult bodies that were also resurrected and taken up to heaven. You cannot imagine the kind of chaos that would ensue upon such a realization.

But someone will argue, "Then what about the nursing mothers that Jesus said will experience dreadful days during the tribulation in Matthew 24:19?" Those are the women who will have babies after the rapture has happened. People will still be having babies, remember!

A Fire Exit

Trust me, you don't want to be left behind to deal with the antichrist and go through the tribulation.

The tribulation will be a time of God's wrath. So the rapture is our "fire exit" from the wrath to come. God does not want us to be judged together with the world, so He has provided **a way of escape** for His people. Jesus Himself said,

> *"Be always on the watch, and **pray that you may be able to escape all** that is about to happen, and **that you may be able to stand before the Son of Man"** (Luke 21:36).

Jesus commands us to be spiritually alert and pray in order that we may escape all that is about to happen. He wants us to be saved from the troubles that are coming on the earth. The other half of the verse has to do with us praying in order that we may be able to stand or appear before the Son of man. This shows us that prayer will play a vital role in determining whether or not we escape these troubles and make it in the rapture.

God always makes a way of escape for His own, but whether they take it or not is up to them. You can be in a burning building, but if you don't take the fire escape you could burn. Do you remember when God wanted to rain fire and brimstone over Sodom and Gomorrah? He sent His angels to **rescue** the godly family of Lot so that they would not be judged with the wicked. The same was true concerning Noah who together with His family **escaped** the great flood that destroyed the people of his generation. In both cases God provided a way of escape for His people before the judgment came.

> Indeed *"if this is so, then the Lord knows how to rescue godly men from trials and to hold the unrighteous for the Day of Judgment..."* (2 Peter2:9a).

Even when it comes to temptation in general, God always provides a way of escape. *"...But when you are tempted, He will also provide a way out so that you can stand up under it"* (1 Corinthians 10:13b).

So the rapture is definitely our escape from the wrath to come as Revelation 3:10 says,

> *"Since you have kept my command to endure patiently, I will also keep you from **the hour of trial** that is going to come upon the **whole world** to test those who live on the earth."*

This hour of trial is the great tribulation that will come upon the whole world. But thank God, you don't have to be a part of it. You can view it all from heaven.

The Wise and Foolish Virgins

Now let us examine what Jesus said in Matthew 25 concerning His return. He had just finished telling His disciples about the dramatic events of the last days in chapter 24. But in chapter 25 He changes the tone and uses three parables to teach them about three prime events yet to happen. These parables are presented in the same sequential order that the events will take place:

- The parable of the ten virgins speaks of the rapture of the church.
- The parable of the talents refers to the Judgment seat of Christ to give an account to the Master and to receive rewards for our labor.
- Then the parable of the sheep and goats speaks of the return of Christ to set up the millennial reign and to judge the nations of the world.

But the underlying message in all three parables is **readiness for His return**. You can remember it as the 4 Rs: Rapture, Rewards and Return calls for Readiness.

Now let's look at the parable of the virgins as it relates to the rapture.

*"At that time the kingdom of heaven will be like ten virgins who took their lamps and went out to meet the bridegroom. Five of them were foolish and five were wise. The foolish ones took their lamps but did not take any oil with them. The wise, however, took oil in jars along with their lamps. The bridegroom was a long time in coming, and they all became drowsy and fell asleep. At midnight the cry rang out; 'Here's the bridegroom! **Come out to meet him!**' Then all the virgins woke up and trimmed their lamps. The foolish ones said to the wise, 'Give us some of your oil; our lamps are going out.' 'No,' they replied, there may not be enough for both us and you. Instead, go to those who sell oil and buy some for yourselves.' But while they were on their way to buy the oil, the bridegroom arrived. The virgins who were **ready** went in with him to the wedding banquet. And the door was shut. Later the others also came. 'Sir! Sir!' they said, 'Open the door for us!' But he replied, "I tell you the truth, I don't know you.' Therefore keep watch, because you do not know the day or the hour"* (Matthew 25:1-13).

Jesus is seen here teaching about the rapture and how to prepare for it. The ten virgins represent the body of Christ (the church) here on earth. They are said to be waiting for the bridegroom. Indeed we are waiting for Jesus to come back. The foolish ones do no take any oil with them meaning that they do not walk in the fullness of the Spirit who is a special envoy sent to prepare us for the coming of the Lord. I must say that the outpouring of the Spirit in these last days is essential to our preparation for His coming. The thing that separated the wise from the foolish was the oil (a type of the Holy Spirit keeping the lamp of their spirit alight and ready to go at a moment's notice).

I believe the lamps in this passage represent their born again human spirits. Proverbs 20:27 (KJV) likens the spirit of man to a lamp: *"The spirit of man is the candle of the Lord..."* A footnote of the NIV rendering of this verse translates it as *"The spirit of man is the Lord's lamp..."* But for this lamp to continue to have light it needs a regular refilling of oil which brings us to the conclusion that the continuous infilling of the Spirit through prayer is essential for our readiness. That is why the baptism in the Holy Spirit is so important. The spirit-filled life is key to being ready when He comes. So you can't expect to live a carnal life all the time and expect to be ready. No, you and I must crucify the flesh and keep it under so we can walk in the spirit ready to go anytime. The bridegroom tells the foolish virgins he never knew them. That means they had not developed an intimate relationship with him. So we must strive to know Him more intimately than any man. It calls for more prayer, more praise and worship to really get to know Him. Like Paul, let us make it our ambition to know Him and to be like Him (Philippians 3:10-11). That's how we'll be ready.

I believe that the move of the Spirit in these last days will culminate in the return of our Lord. Those who do not develop an intimate walk with Him are in danger of missing out on His coming. The foolish virgins are also Christians but they do not walk in the fullness of the Spirit. And so they miss His coming. They are not ready because they have backed away from the Spirit-filled life. Our spiritual intimacy with the Lord determines whether we go or remain. We need to always walk in the Spirit. It is a prerequisite for going in the rapture.

Isaiah Predicts The Rapture?

Some people say that the Old Testament has nothing to say about the rapture. But what do you think about this?:

> *"Thy dead men shall live, together with my dead body shall they arise. Awake and sing, ye that dwell in dust, for thy dew is as the dew of herbs, and the earth shall cast out the dead. **Come, my people, enter thou into thy chambers,** and shut thy doors about thee: **hide thyself as it were for a little moment, until the indignation be overpast.** For behold the Lord cometh out of His place to punish the inhabitants of the earth for their iniquity..."* (Isaiah 26:19-21a).

This is a powerful Old Testament passage that speaks of the resurrection of the dead. And verse 20 paints a beautiful picture of the rapture of the Church as an escape from divine judgment. In verse 21, we actually see the Lord coming to pour out judgment on the inhabitants of the earth. But the Lord has already called His people away to Himself so they don't have to experience His judgment. Praise God!

He says, *"Come, my people, enter thou into thy chambers..."* It is interesting to note how this sounds like what Jesus said in John 14 about His Father's house having many rooms or mansions. The Lord will descend with a shout and call His people away to Himself. The little moment of hiding is the seven year period of tribulation. The raptured Church can stay in heaven until the tribulation or indignation is overpast. So we can rejoice because according to 1 Thessalonians 1:10b He has *"...delivered us from the wrath to come."*

Present-day Benefits of Expecting Christ's Return

Living in the light of Christ's return should affect the way we live our lives each day. It is a powerful motivator for doing what we are required to do knowing that He could come at any moment. So here I have outlined seven of the many benefits that you can experience now as a result of living in the light of His return.

1. Motivation For Holy Living

> *"Dear friends, now we are children of God, and what we will be has not yet been made known. But we know that when He appears, we shall be like Him, for we shall see Him as He is. Everyone who has this hope in him,* **purifies himself***, just as He is pure"* (1 John 3:2-3).

Here we see that looking forward to the rapture inspires us to live holy. This means we need to examine our hearts in the light of His return and allow the Spirit of Sanctification working with the blood and the Word to help us become the glorious church that we are called to be. We must rely on His grace to teach *"us to say 'No' to ungodliness and worldly passions, and to live self-controlled, upright and godly lives in this present age, while we wait for the blessed hope – the glorious appearing of our great God and Savior, Jesus Christ"* (Titus 2:12-13). Through faith we have access to the sanctifying grace of God that empowers us to live holy in this wicked world.

Let us cleanse ourselves from the filth of the world through the blood of Jesus, through the washing of water by the word and through the sanctifying fire of the Holy Spirit. Let us pray the apostolic prayer that God may sanctify us through and through, keeping our whole spirit, soul, and body blameless at the coming of the Lord (1 Thessalonians 5:23). Only by His grace can we be holy in thought, word and deed. We must lay aside every weight that slows us down and the sin that easily entangles so that we can run our spiritual race and finish our course. Remember that sin no longer has dominion over you, for you are not under law but under grace. You are victorious over sin, Satan and temptation.

2. Reason for Fellowship

"Let us not give up meeting together, as some are in the habit of doing, but let us encourage one another – and all the more as you see the day approaching" (Hebrews 10:25).

Looking forward to the coming of Jesus should make us want to spend quality time with believers of like precious faith like ours. Going to church, and other fellowship meetings should be seen as a vital aspect of preparing for His return. The bible says that *"if we walk in the light, as He is in the light, we have fellowship with one another, and the blood of Jesus, his Son, purifies us from all sin"* (1 John 1:7).

That is the power of fellowship, my friends. It will play a vital role in helping us be pure when He comes. So be careful who you associate with. You will become like those you spend quality time with. Light and darkness can not mix. So don't get conformed to this world, for if you do, you may not be prepared to meet Christ at His coming. Minister to the world but don't be part of them. You are in this world but not of this world. I once told a friend that most people don't sin alone. They are usually assisted by someone they associate with. So be careful who you associate with so that they don't affect your chances of going in the rapture.

3. Reason to Maximize Time

"Be very careful, then, how you live – not as unwise but as wise, making the most of every opportunity, because the days are evil" (Ephesians 5:15-16).

Since Jesus could come at any moment, it is vital that we understand how to use our time. We must pray like the Psalmist, *"Teach us to number our days aright, that we may gain a heart of wisdom" (Psalm 90:12).* This wisdom is what will help us to utilize our time in a profitable way for the kingdom. It is what will make us capture opportunities that we would have otherwise wasted. A consciousness of His coming will cause us to be alert so as to employ the resource of time for maximum use. So, let us be good stewards of time so that when He does come, He'll find us investing this resource for His purpose.

4. Motivation for Soul Winning

The most important assignment apart from praying for others is to proclaim and demonstrate the gospel of God's kingdom to the whole world.

> *"And this gospel of the kingdom shall be preached in all the world for a witness unto all nations; and then shall the end come"* (Matthew 24:14 KJV).

Looking forward to the coming of the Lord should be one of the greatest motivations for bringing lost people to Jesus. It should make us want to win more people faster. The assignment to win the lost is directly tied to His appearance. He wants to come and carry a great harvest of souls to heaven. He has been waiting patiently because He wants to give more people opportunity to repent. Therefore our obedience to go out into all the world and preach the gospel will work to speed up the day of His coming. Let us examine ourselves and see the reality of His coming and how it can spur us on to rescue the lost. What a joy it will be for Jesus to find us busy fulfilling His great commission. We shouldn't go to heaven alone. We must carry as many people as possible.

5. Comfort in Suffering

When trials, tribulations and persecutions come, the bible says we should rejoice. Why? Because of what 1 Peter 1:6-7, which says,

> *"In this you greatly rejoice, though for a little while you may have had to suffer grief in all kinds of trials. These*

have come so that your faith – of greater worth than gold, which perishes even though refined by fire – may be proved genuine and may result in praise, glory and honor when Jesus Christ is revealed."

So don't waste your trials grumbling and complaining. See them as opportunities for greater blessing both now and in eternity. If we are persecuted and despised for the cause of Christ we can rejoice that we have been counted worthy to partake of His sufferings.

> *"For our light and momentary troubles are achieving for us an eternal glory that far outweighs them all"* (1 Corinthians 4:17).

It doesn't mean we are to suffer persecution all our life but there will be moments we'll encounter it. Yet it doesn't change the fact that we are overcomers and more than conquerors in Christ. Thank God that every trial is an opportunity to overcome. It is only those who persevere under trial who will receive the crown of life mentioned in James 1:12.

6. Motivation for Service

Anticipating the Lord's return becomes an added incentive for service knowing that our labor in the Lord is not in vain. The Lord has promised to reward us for our service done unto Him.

> *"Behold, I am coming soon! My reward is with me, and I will give to everyone according to what he has done"* (Revelation 22:12).

Those who live this way do not get weary in well doing because they know that pay-day is coming! They work and serve other people as unto the Lord. They give to the poor, assist widows, share the gospel with sinners, all the while fulfilling God's specific calling on their lives with joy. Even their daily duties on the job, at home or at school are done to the glory of God. Indeed they see their whole life as an offering of praise to the Lord. They want to be found serving when their Lord comes.

7. Inspiration for Prayer

> *"Take ye heed, watch and pray: for ye know not when the time is"* (Mark 13:33).

So because Jesus Christ could appear at a moment's notice, our prayer life needs to be in top gear. If we fall asleep spiritually, we may miss His coming. But if we focus on His return we will most certainly be motivated to pray. We must take heed to the Apostle Peter's admonition in 1 Peter 4:7:

> *"The end of all things is near. Therefore be clear-minded and self-controlled so that you can pray."*

Let us live rapture-ready everyday through prayer. Pray for yourself and pray for others.

Now let's pray. This is a Bible-based prayer you can regularly pray:

Father, I thank You for giving me understanding about the coming of the Lord.

May I be like one of the five wise virgins who carried enough oil in their lamps and were ready to meet the bridegroom at His coming.

Father, I pray that I may be counted worthy to escape all that is about to happen and that I may be able to stand before

---

the Son of man.

I ask for grace to walk with You in close [intimate] communion and to know You more than I know any man.

Enable me to be faithful in all that I do and to make the most of every opportunity I have to advance Your kingdom here on earth.

Help me win the lost, heal the sick, help the poor and restore the backslidden. Help me bring all my loved ones to Christ. And I pray that You send forth laborers to those of my relatives I may not personally reach.

Guide me to bring many souls into the Kingdom. Renew my passion for the lost and cause me to labor to do your will and not my own.

I choose to watch and pray as I await your return.

Even so, come Lord Jesus.

Amen

CHAPTER 2

THE JUDGMENT SEAT OF CHRIST

There are four major judgments that are yet to come, each of which will be conducted by our Lord Jesus Christ. The Bible says the Father will judge no man but He has committed all judgment to the Son because He is the Son of Man (John 5:27). So Jesus will be the Chief Justice at every one of the Judgments. **His verdict will be final, irreversible and eternal.**

So brace yourself for a momentous study of these judgments.

1. The Judgment Seat of Christ

> *"For we must all appear before the Judgment Seat of Christ, that each one may receive what is due him for the things done while in the body, whether good or bad"* (1 Corinthians 5:10).

This is a judgment that will take place in heaven immediately after the rapture and is a reward judgment. It is a judgment to reward believers for their works of service while on earth. It is when we will give an account for our lives and receive our due reward. It takes place in heaven and is the first one of the four. The verdict is either a gain or loss of reward. Only godly people will be present at this judgment to receive rewards. It is not a judgment to determine who goes to heaven or hell. All who are present at this judgment are already citizens of heaven, and besides that the judgment itself will take place in heaven. The more we embrace this truth now the better prepared we can be.

2. The Judgment of the Nations

> *"Then the King will say to those on His right, 'Come, you who are blessed by my Father; take your inheritance, the*

Kingdom prepared for you since the creation of the world.' Then He will say to those on His left, 'Depart from me, you who are cursed, into the eternal fire prepared for the devil and His angels'" (Matthew 25:34, 41).

The Judgment of the Nations takes place on earth when Jesus comes back to set up the millennial reign. The saints who faced the Judgment Seat of Christ will also return with Him. All the nations will be gathered before Him and He will separate them into two groups: one called the sheep and the other the goats. The sheep are the ones deemed worthy to enter the millennial kingdom while the goats are sentenced to eternal fire. This happens at the end of the seven year tribulation period which these two groups have survived. So before Jesus can set up the millennial reign He has to qualify the natural inhabitants of the millennial kingdom.

3. The Judgment of Israel

The Judgment of Israel also takes place on earth just before or immediately following the Judgment of the Nations (the Gentiles). The whole nation of Israel will be brought to its knees as it recognizes Jesus as the true Messiah that they had rejected.

> *"...They will look on me, the one they have pierced, and they will mourn for Him as one mourns for an only child, and grieve bitterly for Him as one grieves for a first born son"* (Zechariah 12:10b).

This will be a time of national mourning when the whole nation of Israel will return to God. After that, the millennial reign can begin.

4. The Great White Throne Judgment

The Great White Throne Judgment is probably the most fearsome of them all. This will be a judgment of all the wicked dead who have died since the time of Adam. This judgment takes place after the millennial reign of Christ (a period of 1,000 years when Christ will rule the earth with His saints). It is not a lovely sight to behold and must be avoided at all costs. My friend, you don't want to be there. The verdict is too ghastly to contemplate. This will be the final abode of the wicked: a lake of fire and brimstone burning forever and ever and ever. I warn you, don't take a chance to go there. Make sure your life is right with God today. Repent and pray to Him. **Pray for salvation now**! This fire was not created for man but it's unfortunate that some people will follow Satan there. Don't play games with God my friend, this terrible punishment will last forever – no escape, no relief…forever. Read it for yourself:

> *"Then I saw a great white throne and Him who was seated on it. Earth and sky fled from His presence, and there was no place for them. And I saw the dead, great and small, standing before the throne, and books were opened. Another book was opened, which is the Book of Life. The dead were judged according to what they had done as recorded in the books. The sea gave up the dead that were in it, and death and Hades gave up the dead that were in them, and each person was judged according to what he had done. Then Death and Hades were thrown into the lake of fire. The lake of fire is the second death. If anyone's name was not found written in the Book of Life, he was thrown into the lake of fire"* (Revelation 20:11-15).

I am not for scaring people into heaven. My responsibility is to warn this world that there is an eternal place of torment called hell that you don't have to go to. It is furthermore my pleasure to invite every inhabitant of this planet to receive Jesus Christ who alone is the way to heaven. I cannot think of something more tragic than a lost soul in hell. An eternally lost soul has to be the most tragic thing to ever hit God's creation. The bottom line of my message is this: **there's a heaven to aspire for and a hell to shun. Therefore, you choose where you will spend eternity!**

Accountability

Now let's take a critical look at the Judgment Seat of Christ. This may not be the most popular subject, but it's one of the most important. It is certainly a sobering truth, but it's also a liberating one. It will remove spiritual laziness and help you get prepared so that you can give a worthy account of your life to Him. Romans 14:12 says, *"So then every one of us shall give an account of himself to God."*

That's an awesome thought isn't it? I believe that each of us should begin to live our lives in the light of that day. It will certainly change the way we look at life and help us make the necessary adjustments that we need to make. No student wants to fail an exam and no accountant wants to fail an audit. Our lives will be examined and audited to determine whether we get a reward or not.

1 Corinthians 3:12-15 gives us a glimpse of the possible results we can expect on that great day.

> *"Now if any man build upon this foundation gold, silver, precious stones, wood, hay, stubble; Every man's work shall be made manifest: for the day shall declare it, because it shall be revealed by fire; and the fire shall try every man's work of what sort it is. If any man's work abide which he built thereupon, he shall receive a reward. If any man's work shall be burned, he shall suffer loss: but he himself shall be saved; yet so as by fire."*

Now if we connect this passage with 2 John 8 we get a fuller picture of the three possible results at the Judgment Seat of Christ. It says, *"Watch out that you do not lose what you have worked for, but that you may be rewarded fully"* (2 John 8).

So the three possible results are as follows:

1. No Reward

1 Corinthians 3:15 tells us, *"If any man's work shall be burned, he shall suffer loss..."* There is clearly no reward for this believer. He just barely made it to heaven. He has not fulfilled God's purpose while on earth but lived for himself. So his verdict at the judgment seat of Christ is: no reward! His examination record shows 0%. He will be a commoner in heaven – no crown, no throne. The bible says some people will be called least in the kingdom of heaven (Matthew 5:19).

2. Partial Reward

The warning in 2 John 8, *"Watch out that you do not lose what you have worked for,"* implies that it is possible to get only part of the reward you were supposed to get had you served to your fullest. It is just like examination grades: you can get a distinction or a lesser grade. You are graded according to your performance.

The first part of that verse tells you to *"Watch out that you do not lose what you have worked for..."* So could it be possible that some people tend to cancel out some of their reward through perpetual disobedience? Revelation 3:11 gives us the same warning:

> *"I am coming soon. Hold on to what you have, so that no one will take your crown."*

I certainly don't want anybody taking my crown! How about you? Later on we'll be looking at the parable of the talents where the wicked servant's talent was taken away from him and given to someone who had gained five more. We cannot afford to be careless. Why let someone take your crown?

3. Full Reward

According to 2 John verse 8, a full reward is a possibility for all those who serve faithfully. God is not unfair. He has made it possible for everyone of His children to attain the highest mark in relation to their own calling. We are all called to do different things, but the reward we get will depend on how faithful we were to the assignment we were given. You can't just live your life for self. You need to get on your knees and find out what God's assignment is for you. Know what God has called you to do and fulfill that assignment. A pastor who is faithful in fulfilling his pastoral assignment will not be rewarded more than an usher or praying mother who faithfully served God from the heart. Their functions are different and their rewards are based on obedience and faithfulness to the call. God will not reward positions, He will reward faithfulness. So let's aim for a full reward. Remember, the verdict at the Judgment Seat of Christ determines who you become forever – a king or less than a king. The choice is yours.

Listen! You are better off facing this hard truth now, and making adjustments than to suffer loss at the Judgment Seat of Christ. So get ready for a lifestyle of change. Be transformed and become everything God created you to be.

The Parable of the Talents

Now let's visit with Jesus again and see what He has to say on the matter of rewards. The parable of the talents in Matthew 25:14-30 is a clear-cut teaching of what will happen at the judgment seat of Christ.

The three servants had been entrusted with talents (amounts of money), each according to his abilities. The one who got five talents invested it and gained five more, bringing his total to ten. The one who got two also invested it and gained two more, bringing his total to four. But the one who got one talent did not invest it but rather hid it much to his disadvantage.

So when the Master returned to settle accounts with them, he gave the same commendation or reward to the first two servants.

"His master replied, Well done, good and **faithful** *servant! You have been* **faithful** *with a few things; I will put you in charge of many things. Come and share your master's happiness"* (Matthew 25:21, 23).

That is an example of those who will get a full reward even if their earthly responsibilities were not equal. They'll be rewarded based on their faithfulness to the call of God on their life.

The third servant also came and his master had this to say:

"...You wicked, lazy servant...Take the talent from him and give it to the one who has the ten talents. For everyone who has will be given more, and he will have an abundance. Whoever does not have, even what he has will be taken from him. And throw that worthless servant outside, into darkness, where there will be weeping and gnashing of teeth" (Matthew 25:26, 28-30).

The master is clearly upset with this servant and instructs his attendants to strip him of the one talent that he has and give it to the one with ten. Could this be a picture of the unfaithful unproductive Christian losing his reward to a good and faithful servant? Could this be what Jesus was talking about when he said, *"I am coming soon. Hold on to what you have, so that no one will take your crown?"* (Revelation 3:11). So we can't afford to be unproductive; it could cost us more than we are willing to pay!

Now I know that Matthew 25:30 has bothered a lot of people because they think it refers to being sent to hell. But it actually doesn't. It refers to the lowest position or rank in the kingdom of heaven where the least people are – commoners in other words. The phrase *"...outside, into darkness, where there will be weeping and gnashing of teeth"* refers to a low place of regret, considering you could have done better. It is simply a word picture of the remorse that follows a bad performance at the Judgment Seat of Christ. This regret will only be experienced during the judgment but joy will be the eternal experience of this soul.

Like I said before, this person just barely made it to heaven and was only saved by the skin of his teeth. Perhaps that's why he's gnashing them! Nevertheless, his experience of heaven will still be blissful but he'll miss out on certain privileges and responsibilities that he could have had. I don't want this to happen to me. How about you?

Reflection

Now think about your life today. Do you want your works to burn and barely make it to heaven? What adjustments can you make in your own spiritual life with regard to His coming? What aspects of your life need some fine tuning? Is there any need for repentance? Take some time to pray today and ask God to help you. Also read through chapters 2 and 3 of the book of Revelation over and over for a few days. Let the messages to the seven churches minister life to you so that you can better prepare for His return. It is essential that we pray like the Apostle Paul:

> *"And this is my prayer: that your love may abound more and more in knowledge and depth of insight, so that you may be able to discern what is best and may be pure and blameless until the day of Christ, filled with the fruit of righteousness that comes through Jesus Christ – to the glory and praise of God"* (Philippians 1:9). *"May God Himself, the God of peace, sanctify you through and through. May your whole spirit, soul and body be kept blameless at the coming of our Lord Jesus Christ"* (1 Thessalonians 5:23)

You can personalize these prayers and pray them often for yourself and others inserting your name or someone else's name where it says "your" and "you."

Are You Ready For The Master?

"Be dressed ready for service and keep your lamps burning, like men waiting for their master to return from a wedding banquet, so that when he comes and knocks, they can immediately open the door for him. It will be good for those servants whose master finds them watching when he comes...You also must be ready, because the Son of Man will come at an hour when you do not expect Him" (Luke 12:35-37b, 40)

So what happens if you are not ready? It is the same thing that happens when you are not at the airport when your plane is scheduled to fly. The pilot will not wait for you. You should have been waiting for him!

All of us Christians are called to serve in one capacity or another. It is our responsibility to make ourselves ready for service and to keep our lamps (spirits) burning with the fire of the Holy Spirit. You notice that when the master knocks, He expects the servant to immediately open the door for him. That shows that he is ever alert and on guard until the master comes. And as Jesus puts it, *"It will be good for those servants whose master finds them watching when he comes"* (Luke 12:37a). They must be ready because their master can show up at any moment.

Tired of Waiting?

The discourse takes a turn in Luke 12:45 when one of the servants gets tired of waiting. Let's read Luke 12:45 to 48.

*"But suppose the servant says to himself, 'My master is **taking a long time in coming**; and he then begins to*

*beat the menservants and maidservants and to eat and drink and get drunk. The master of that servant will come on a day when he does not expect him and at an hour he is not aware of. He will cut him to pieces and assign him a place with the unbelievers. That servant who knows his master's will and **does not get ready or does not do** what his master wants will be beaten with **many blows**. But the one who does not know and does things deserving punishment will be beaten with few blows. From everyone who has been **given much, much will be demanded**; and from the one who has been **entrusted with much, much more will be asked.**"*

Disobedience has consequences. You cannot disobey the call of God and expect to please your Maker! In the passage we've just read, Jesus reveals the fate that will befall the disobedient Christian.

In verse 45 we see the servant beginning to get tired of waiting for his master and beating up (persecuting and working against) his fellow servants. We even see him begin to drink and get drunk in stead of being sober so he can watch and pray. I don't know the exact nature of this particular servant's fate. But whatever it is, **it's a costly one!** It is the master's prerogative to make a just judgment.

The Lord will hold us accountable for **His will**. He will ask if we fulfilled His will not our own. We must pray and find out what that will is and prepare to do it or we will suffer loss. God's will is the purpose for which He created us. The servant who knows his master's will but does not do It Is held accountable for what he knows. The servant who does not know his master's will faces consequences in relation to his ignorance. His sentence is more lenient but still very costly. He may just barely make it to heaven with no reward. You had better watch out!

The statement in verse 45 is a bombshell: *"From everyone who has been given much, much will be demanded; and from the one who has been entrusted with much, much more will be asked."*

God is a God of accountability. He will demand much from those He's given much and much more from those He's entrusted with a lot more.

Reflection

Do you know God's specific will for your life? Are you getting ready to fulfill it? Are you doing what the Master wants or you are just doing your own thing?

You can't afford to be ignorant of His will. It can cost you your reward. Making it to heaven is certainly wonderful beyond description. Yet it's even more glorious when you have rewards. We must take responsibility for our lives here and now so that we can make our mark on eternity! **You don't have to make history: You just need to impact eternity!** If you live to make history, your accomplishments will pass away. But if you live to impact eternity, your kingdom achievements will be rewarded and remembered forever.

Let's Pray

The following prayer is based on the prayers in the New Testament and deals with God's will for your life. Pray it often until you discover and fulfill God's purpose for your life.

Dear Heavenly Father, I ask You to give me the Spirit of wisdom and revelation, so that I may know You better. I pray also that the eyes of my heart may be enlightened in order that I may know the hope to which You have called me, the riches of your glorious inheritance in the saints and Your incomparably great power for me who believes (Ephesians 1:16-20).

Faithful Father, I pray that You may equip me with

everything good for doing your will and that You may work in me what is pleasing to You through Christ Jesus (Hebrews 13:20-21).

I pray this so that the name of our Lord Jesus may be glorified in me, and me in Him, according to the grace of our God and the Lord Jesus Christ 2 Thessalonians 1:11-12).

I pray that I may stand firm in all the will of God, mature and fully assured
(Colossians 4:12).

Now Father, fill me with the knowledge of Your will through all spiritual wisdom and understanding, that I may walk worthy of the Lord, fully pleasing Him, being fruitful in every good work and increasing in the knowledge of God (Colossians 1:9-10).

Thy will be done on earth in my life as it is in heaven (Matthew 6:10).

In Jesus' name I pray.

Amen.

"But if anyone builds upon the Foundation, whether it be with gold, silver, precious stones, wood, hay, straw, the work of each [one] will become [plainly, openly] known (shown for what it is); for the day [of Christ] will disclose and declare it, because it will be revealed with fire, and the fire will test and critically appraise the character and worth of the work each person has done. If the work which any person has built on this Foundation [any product of his efforts whatever] survives [this test], he will get his reward.

But if any person's work is burned up [under the test], he will suffer loss [of it all, losing his reward], though he himself will be saved, but only as [one who has passed] through fire."

(1 Corinthians 3:12-15 AMP)

This Was Your Life

The day is coming when we shall give an account of our lives at the Judgment Seat of Christ. Our lives will be laid bare before Him for evaluation. Our works will be examined to determine their worth. If deemed worthy we'll get a reward. If not we won't.

So, what will this evaluation actually include? It will include every aspect of our lives but here I have tried to codify those aspects into 10 divisions. Take time to evaluate yourself in these areas and increase your chances for success on that day! Do your best while you have the opportunity.

1. Our Relationship with God

How close or intimate we are to God will be of paramount importance at the Judgment Seat of Christ. Remember that to love the Lord Your God with all your heart, soul, mind and strength is the greatest commandment of all (Mark 12:28-31). And here's a reward for it: *"Blessed is the man that endureth temptation: for when he is tried, he shall receive the crown of life, which the Lord has promised to those that love Him"* (James 1:12 KJV).

Evaluate your relationship with God today and get to know Him better through His Word and by spending quality time praising and worshipping Him. Make it a top priority to know Him intimately day by day. As the Apostle Paul said, *"That I may know Him, and the power of His resurrection, and the fellowship of His sufferings, being made conformable unto His death"* (Philippians 3:10). There is no greater quest than to know Him intimately. Make it your number one priority in life.

Think of Enoch and Moses who knew God intimately. Think of the Apostle Paul and Jesus Himself Who fellowshipped with the Father most intimately. You can have it if you want it. But you must do what it takes to walk in it. Pray, praise and worship Him. Spend time meditating on God's word and focus on Him daily. How close you are to Him on earth will determine how close you will seat with Him in heaven. Our highest calling is to abide in Him and let Him abide in us (John 15:4-7). God wants fellowship with you more than anything else. That's why He created you.

2. Our Relationships with Others

How well we treat other people will to a large degree determine how well we fare on that day. You see, people are created in the image of God and you can't just treat them any way you like. We all know the New Testament command given to us by the Lord Jesus to love one another as He has loved us (John 15:12). Therefore it is imperative that we treat people right. It is not for us to criticize or judge them. Ours is to love and bless. We are to treat even our enemies with kindness. It's not just a matter of enduring abuse. It's a matter of overcoming through love and gaining rewards thereby.

> *"But I say unto you: Love your enemies, bless them that curse you, do good to them that hate you, and pray for them which despitefully use you, and persecute you – For if ye love them which love you, what reward have you? Do not even the publicans the same?"* (Matthew 5:44, 46 KJV).

We will do well to follow the golden rule: Do to others what you would have them do to you. (Matthew 7:12) In other words, be proactive in exercising love. Initiate the action in loving others. Don't wait for others to love you first. Go ahead and love them first. So as far as it depends on us, let us live at peace with all men (Romans 12:18).

3. Our Prayer life

Prayer is one of the greatest works we can ever do to advance the kingdom of God on earth. I personally believe that some of the people with the greatest rewards in heaven are faithful intercessors. Our nations need prayer. Our leaders need prayer. Our churches need prayer. It's hard to even imagine an area of our lives that doesn't need prayer to move forward. Prayer is indispensible when it comes to doing God's will. Nothing advances God's will more than prayer. Just take a look at Jesus. He could have never accomplished God's will without much prayer! He had to hear from God. He had to know what to do for each day.

So how is your prayer life? Do you even have a prayer life? O saint, do something to make prayer a regular part of your life. Let prayer become the respiratory system of your spiritual life. Yes, we will be held accountable for our prayer life. *"As for me far be it from me that I should sin against the Lord by failing to pray for you..."* (1 Samuel 12:23a). The Lord wants us to pray God's will to pass. He wants us to hold fast to prayer until God's will is done. May we all take heed to God's word in 1 Timothy 2:1-3:

> *"I urge, then, first of all, that requests, prayers, intercession and thanksgiving be made for everyone – for kings and all those in authority, that we may live peaceful and quiet lives in all godliness and holiness. This is good, and pleases God our Savior, who wants all men to be saved and to come to a knowledge of the truth."*

Let prayer become the respiratory system of your spiritual life.

4. The Will of God for Our Life

What has God called you to do? Have you asked Him to show you His plan for your life? Or are you living a life without purpose? Friend, you cannot afford to merely exist. Find out the reason why you are here. Pray and fast if necessary until you get a clear picture of what your assignment is. And when you discover it, get down to work!

The Bible says, *"For the gifts and calling of God are without repentance"* (Romans 11:29). That means that God will never change His mind about what He has called you to do. He will not withdraw His specific assignment for you but will require it at the judgment. He will call you to account for the gifts and calling that He gave you before you were born (Jeremiah 1:5). Our gifts are given to us to help us fulfill our calling. It is not enough to merely do good works. We must do God-ordained good works – the works that God created us to do. *"For we are God's workmanship, created in Christ Jesus to do good works, which God prepared in advance for us to do"* (Ephesians 2:10).

So, find out God's will or your life will be lived in vain. Psalm 127:1 says, *"Except the Lord build the house, they labor in vain that build it..."* If anything in your life is not built according to the design of His purpose for you, it is all in vain. It's a pile of wood, hay and sticks that will burn to ashes on that day when our works are tested. You must find out God's will and build in line with it.

You must settle for nothing less than the perfect will of God for your life (Romans 12:1-2). Let us be like Jesus who was so passionate for God's will that He could hardly eat. *"My food, said Jesus, is to do the will of Him who sent me and to finish His work"* (John 4:34). Our goals and aspirations in life must be in line with God's will. Make no major decision without consulting Him. God will ask you whether you did His will or your own. The answer to that question will determine your eternal position with Him.

5. Our Stewardship of Resources

> *"Moreover, it is required in stewards, that a man be found faithful"* (1 Corinthians 4:2).

God has entrusted us with valuable resources to use in His service. The resources of time, talents and treasure are a great part of our stewardship calling. We must learn how to manage our time, develop our talents and use our treasure for the extension of God's kingdom on earth.

Are you investing your time in God's service? Are you making the most of every opportunity? God will hold us accountable for every opportunity that was wasted. Have you discovered your gifts, talents and abilities? Are you using them for the glory of His name or simply for your fame? Are you a good steward of money and other possessions? Are you using your money to support your local church, help the poor or send out missionaries? Let us be wise stewards who will do the best with what we have and make it count on that day. Take time to ask God how best you can employ your talents, invest your time and spend your treasures for the advancement of His will on earth. Don't take what you have too personally. See it as entrusted to you to serve His purposes because one day you will give an account to the Owner. Don't waste time. Don't let your gifts lie dormant. Never waste money or possessions. Use them for the glory of the King. Make your time, talents and treasure count for eternity.

6. Our Witness

Every believer ought to be a soul winner. We are called to be salt and light to the world. We are representatives of the King of kings – Christ's ambassadors. We have an ambassadorial responsibility to win souls for Him. *"All this is from God, who reconciled us to Himself through Christ and gave us the ministry of reconciliation"* (2 Corinthians 5:18). We are to reconcile men to God through Christ. We are called to be witnesses for Jesus. Every soul is valuable to God and He wants it saved. He wants us to reach out on His behalf to bring men to Him. Our relatives, our workmates, our schoolmates and our friends all need Jesus. Jesus wants heaven full. He wants to present an innumerable company of saints to the Father.

He died for these souls and He will require their blood at our hands. He will hold us accountable for the lost because we had the message but we didn't preach, we had the opportunity but we didn't reach. Are we doing enough to save the lost? Or is it something we think only the preacher should do? No, it's the job of every one of us to be reapers in the Lord's harvest field. In fact that's why He's even delaying His coming because *"...He is patient with you, not wanting anyone to perish, but everyone to come to repentance"* (1 Peter 3:9).

The Bible says that there is rejoicing in heaven over one sinner who repents. The value of a soul is incalculable. It is worth the blood of Jesus. Jesus wants to reap a harvest for the suffering that He went through on the cross. Let us awaken a passion for the lost by asking God to help us. Let us repent of our indifference and non-caring attitude so that we can win souls for Him. They are the greatest thing we can ever carry to heaven of all our works. And by the way, there's a special crown to be given only to soul winners. In fact Daniel tells us that *"Those who are wise will shine like the brightness of the heavens, and those who lead many to righteousness, like the stars forever and ever"* (Daniel 12:3). That is the glory of soul winning my friends! Ask God for wisdom, and boldness to rescue souls from a burning hell. We can't leave the job to the evangelist alone. Let us do our part and look forward to a soul winner's crown on that day. *"...he who wins souls is wise"* (Proverbs 11:30). Remember, you have a ministry of reconciliation. Have you done some ambassadorial work lately? It's time to wake up to the call to go and make disciples of all nations. That's our great commission as ambassadors for the kingdom.

7. Our Motives

"Therefore judge nothing before the appointed time; wait till the Lord comes. He will bring to light what is hidden in darkness and will expose the motives of men's hearts. At that time each will receive his praise from God" (1 Corinthians 4:5).

What is the motive behind what you do? Is it to receive honor from men or commendation from God? It is one thing to do the right thing, but it's totally another to do it with the right motive. The value of your works before God is determined by the motive behind them. Anything done for show so that men can see is a work of wood, hay and straw that will burn to ashes on that day. But any good work done out of love to glorify the Father will be rewarded even if it's just giving a cup of cold water to a thirsty disciple (Matthew 10:42). You see, it's not how big your actions are, it's how loving they are. Your motives are of utmost importance to God.

The bible teaches that without love all your actions are worthless. They may seem good to people but they are of no value to God. They may impress men but they won't get God's approval. That's why it's important that we weigh our motives in His presence and allow God's word to judge them (Hebrews 4:12). We need to constantly surrender and yield our desires to Him so that we can have His heart on every matter. We need to live motivated by His Word, His Spirit and His love. We can only accomplish that by continually abiding in Him. If we abide in Him and His word abides in us, His desires will become ours and those desires will produce actions in line with God's thoughts motivated by His love. God is love and everything He does is motivated by love. Make it a priority to do everything you do out of love – your praying, giving, service and even your house work!

Without love you are nothing. Without love you gain nothing. Love is the master key to eternal rewards. *"If I give all I posses to the poor and surrender my body to the flames, but have not love, I gain nothing"* (1 Corinthians 13:3). But if I do it out of love, I gain a reward that will never fade away.

There will be no reward for any deed done with ulterior motives. But whatever we do to glorify the Father will be rewarded fully. Let us allow the sword of the Spirit to correct the thoughts and motives of our heart so that we can serve Him with a pure heart. *"For the word of God is living and active. Sharper than any double-edged sword, it penetrates even to dividing soul and spirit, joints and marrow; it judges the thoughts and attitudes of the heart"* (Hebrews 4:12). We usually read this verse and end here thinking, 'Wow, what a scripture!' But the next verse continues the discourse and concludes with the day of accountability. It reads, *"Nothing in all creation is hidden from God's sight. Everything is uncovered and laid bare before the eyes of Him to Whom we must give account"* (Hebrews 4:13).

Folks, let us not allow pride, envy, competition or covetousness to motivate us in anything we do. We shouldn't let selfishness motivate us to gain at the expense of others. In Philippians 2:3 we are admonished to *"Do nothing out of selfish ambition or vain conceit, but in humility consider others better than yourselves."*

Let us seek the honor from above, not the praises of men.

Love is the master key to eternal rewards.

8. Our Words

Words are far more powerful than we ever thought they were. They have eternal consequences for good or for bad that are incalculable.

The Bible admonishes us to let no corrupt communication come out of our mouths but only that which is helpful for building others up (See Ephesians 4:29). We are to listen twice as much as we speak. I understand that's why God gave us two ears and only one mouth. We are to be quick to listen, slow to speak, and slow to become angry (James 1:19).

Why does God place such a high premium on words? For one, words are the means through which God created all things. So it stands to reason that they have a profound impact on our lives. Words have the creative potential for good or evil. They can do more damage than sticks or stones. When used improperly they become arrows that wound deeply. Wrong words will be judged. The Bible even says that idle words will have to be accounted for. These are words that we speak carelessly from day to day.

This basically means that our integrity will be weighed in a balance. These include unfulfilled promises we are always fond of making. To be people of integrity we should learn to keep our word just as God keeps His. Because we are made in His image, we should imitate Him by watching over our word to perform it. Integrity must be seen in our being punctual at work, following through on our financial pledges and being faithful with everyday promises and commitments among other things.

The bible speaks of other books besides the book of life which will be opened at the judgment. These books are records of our thoughts, words and deeds. These records will be the basis on which we will be judged besides the bible itself. God will hold us accountable for idle words, but He will also reward us for using our words aright. Your words will cost or gain you rewards in heaven. This is not something I'm making up. This is sober truth. *"But I tell you that men will have to give account on the Day of Judgment for every careless word they have spoken. For by your words you will be acquitted, and by your words you will be condemned"* (Matthew 12:36-37)

I'd like to picture the books from which we'll be judged as Book 1: Thoughts, Book 2: Words, and Book 3: Deeds. Now imagine with me the volume or size of each book. How big could your books be by now? Friend, you and I need to examine the words we speak or they could cost us on that day. We must refrain our tongue from criticizing, judging, or condemning others. We must keep our tongue from evil. Instead let us train ourselves to speak good so that what we say is recorded to our advantage as Malachi 3:16 reveals:

"Then they that feared the Lord spake often one to another: and the Lord hearkened, and heard it, and a book of remembrance was written before Him for them that feared the Lord and thought upon His name."

Therefore our prayer should be:

> *May the WORDS of my mouth and the MEDITATION of my heart be pleasing in your sight, O Lord, my Rock and my Redeemer. Psalm 19:14*

It's time to repent of every negative word and make things right with God. We must then resolve to speak what is helpful for others to hear and not what tears them down. Remember, it's a matter of win or lose at the Judgment Seat of Christ.

9. Our Deeds

What may constitute a bad deed at the Judgment Seat of Christ may not necessarily be an evil thing we did but rather a good action with the wrong motives. The Lord will weigh our acts based on the motive of our heart. If our good deeds are done to gain the praise and adoration of men they will have to burn to ashes. But if what we do is based on His love, to glorify His holy name, it will survive the fire and produce a reward.

The consequences of our actions – good or bad – will be brought to light on that day. For example, if you behave in such a way that your actions cause a baby Christian to stumble or turn away from God, then you will be held responsible for their failure. We must never facilitate for others to sin or we will be counted party with them.

The Lord will evaluate our acts of service. The bible says that the actions that we do for men as unto the Lord will be considered done for Jesus. If we give to the poor, visit those in prison, care for widows and orphans, honor our parents, guardians and those in authority and do a fine job at home and at work to the glory of God, we will be rewarded richly for our service. But if we do the same things with the wrong motives, we will lose our reward. This is so important because our works of service and our behavioral acts will constitute our garments in heaven. *"Fine linen, bright and clean, was given her to wear. (Fine linen stands for the righteous acts of the saints)"* (Revelation 19:8). So we will wear designer clothes in heaven designed by the actions of our lives on earth. Our deeds of service will make up the material for our garments in heaven.

Other than the souls you win, there is something else you will carry with you to heaven. *"Then I heard a voice from heaven say, Write: Blessed are the dead who die in the Lord from now on. Yes says the Spirit, they will rest from their labour, for their deeds will follow them"* (Revelation 14:13). Our good works will follow us into eternity. No work of service will go unnoticed if it is done as unto the Lord. Even for the employees, don't just work for a salary or pension, but do your job as unto the Lord and you can expect a real pay day that day!

Some will be called to account for more than others because of their greater influence on others. Parents, employers, church leaders, political leaders, and leaders in various fields will have to account for the influence they had on others for good or bad. So, treat the people you lead with respect or it could cost you rewards.

We are not saved by our works, but we are saved to do good works that God requires. *"For we are God's workmanship, created in Christ Jesus to do good works, which God prepared in advance for us to do"* (Ephesians 2:10).

Yet there's another aspect of the judgment that has to do with the things we did not do that we should and could have done. For example, if we had an opportunity to help someone and we turned them away even though we had the means, we will have to account for our refusal to help. Our neglect of responsibility will cost us on that day. So make your every action count for eternity. Your job as a sweeper, house maid, cook, garden boy, accountant or CEO is of great importance before God. If you do it as unto the Lord, you will be rewarded for it. *"Anyone, then, who knows the good he ought to do and doesn't do it, sins"* (James 4:17).

10. Our Priorities

Have you put God first in your life? Is He first in your marriage, your career, your finances and your decision-making? What is the greatest object for which you are living? Is it to glorify His name or to amplify yours?

"But seek first His kingdom and His righteousness, and all these things will be given to you as well" (Matthew 6:33). If you make God and His kingdom the number one priority in your life, you will have done well. God cannot occupy second place. He must be first. His word must guide your actions and govern your every decision. Your highest ambition, your greatest aim, and your hottest pursuit should be to know Him and to serve Him. If that is not the case, then whatever is occupying first place in your life is an idol.

David had one thing that he wanted the most. Psalm 27:4 tells us what it is: *"One thing I ask of the Lord, this is what I seek: that I may dwell in the house of the Lord all the days of my life, to gaze upon the beauty of the Lord and to seek Him in His temple."* That was David's number one priority. What's yours?

Is it to make lots of money? There's nothing wrong with making money as long as it doesn't take first place in your life. Settle it in your heart today to put first things first. Our priorities must be in line with God's priorities.

Questions You Could Expect At the Judgment Seat of Christ

1. Did you follow your own plan or My plan for your life?

2. What did you do about the gifts and callings of God on your life?

3. Did you consult Me on the major decisions you made?

4. Did you use your gifts and talents to glorify Me or to further your own causes?

5. Is this the best you could have done or you were more capable than this?

6. What was the motive for doing what you did?

7. Was I top priority in your life?

8. Can you account for the time and money that I gave you?

9. Were you a faithful employee? Were you a fair employer?

10. Did you pray for your President, Government and nation faithfully?

11. How did you treat people who didn't like you?

12. Did you use your influence for good or for evil?

13. How did you handle the people I sent to you for help?

14. Were you ashamed of Me and My gospel before men?

15. Did you take the time to teach your children My ways?

16. Did you support you local church and pastor faithfully with your money, prayers and service?

17. What was the main cause you lived for?

18. Did you win and disciple souls for Me?

19. Did you seek to please men or to please Me?

20. Were your works done out of love to glorify Me or for selfish motives?

21. How did you treat your spouse and children?

22. How did you treat the relatives (and in-laws) I gave to you?

23. What example did you set for others to follow?

24. Did you put into practice the Word of God that you learned?

These and other such questions need to be settled if we ever hope to perform well on that day. So pray and let the Holy Spirit help you realign your life in line with God's will.

Examine yourself to see whether you are in the faith. Humble yourself and make the necessary adjustments. Surrender and consecrate yourself to Him and His purposes for your life.

The Verdict

The verdict at the Judgment Seat of Christ will be final, irreversible and eternal. There will be no appeal to a higher court because there is no higher court. The sentence pronounced will forever fix your position in the eternal kingdom. You will find out whether you are a king or not.

Jesus once said that the Father judges no man, but that He has entrusted all judgment to the Son because He is the Son of man (John 5:22-27). You can be sure of one thing: The judgment will be absolutely fair! It will be a transparent and righteous judgment based on the truth of the Word of God which is able to judge the thoughts and hidden motives of the heart. There can be no favoritism with Him. It will be the most righteous judgment ever.

This judgment like I've said before is not a judgment of sinners but of Christians. It is a judgment of those who already know Jesus Christ as their Lord and Savior. The purpose of it is to determine their eternal rewards.

The "Heavenly Big Screen" will show the DVD of your life – your thoughts, your words and your deeds. You will give your account and the verdict will be delivered. Can you see yourself standing there looking in the face of your Righteous Judge? The record of your life is reviewed and the Lord announces the decision. Will it be a rebuke or a commendation? Your current life has everything to do with it.

Now imagine if you appeared before the Judgment Seat this very moment. Do you suppose the verdict will be in your favor or not? Are you concerned that your works would burn? My friend, think seriously about this. Don't waste your life on what's temporal. Focus on what's eternal and you'll never live to regret the verdict.

Judgment in Your Favor

When most people hear the word judgment they immediately think of wrath, anger and punishment. That is one side of the story. Another side is what I call judgment in your favor. This is when the judge pronounces a sentence that favors you. Such a sentence becomes a cause for rejoicing.

There're so many positive aspects to the judgments of God, it's amazing. For example, God the Father judged Jesus on the cross for our sins. He took our judgment so that we could be set free. He became our substitute in a case we had lost and served our sentence for us. We have now been declared righteous in Christ. That was judgment in our favor.

So even at the Judgment Seat of Christ, there will be people who will be rewarded without rebuke. While others will have some rebuke and some reward. But then there are others who will only receive rebuke and no reward. The Lord will give each one what he is due for the things done in the body whether good or bad.

> *"And now dear children, continue in Him, so that when He appears we may be confident and unashamed before Him at His coming"* (1 John 2:28).

> *"He will keep you strong to the end, so that you will be blameless on the day of our Lord Jesus Christ"* (1 Corinthians 1:8).

> *"May He strengthen your hearts so that you will be blameless and holy in the presence of our God and Father when our Lord Jesus comes with all his holy ones"* (1 Thessalonians 3:13).

Jesus is washing His church through the agency of the word so that He may *"...present her to Himself as a radiant church, without stain or wrinkle or any other blemish, but holy and blameless"* (Ephesians 5:27). So let's yield to the cleansing process and become the glorious church that He wants.

CHAPTER 3

HEAVENLY REWARDS

Worldly accolades cannot even begin to compare with the eternal crowns and other rewards to be given at the Judgment Seat of Christ. Grammys, Oscars, World Cups, and Olympic Medals pale in comparison with even the least reward in eternity. The Nobel Peace Prize is reduced to a common artifact in comparison with any one of the heavenly crowns. Why would anybody forfeit the great privilege of attaining a heavenly reward? Can you hear the voice of Jesus saying, *"I am coming soon. Hold on to what you have, so that no one will take your crown?"* (Revelation 3:11).

Your attitude should be like this: *"Not that I have already obtained all this, or have already been made perfect, but I press on to take hold of that for which Christ took hold of me. Brothers, I do not consider myself yet to have taken hold of it. But one thing I do: Forgetting what is behind and straining toward what is ahead, I press on toward the goal to win the prize for which God has called me heavenward in Christ Jesus"* (Philippians 3:12-14).

Let us not be like Esau who sold his birthright for a bowl of lentils. He lost his firstborn status and the blessing that he was supposed to inherit. He put carnal things before spiritual and eternal things. He is a classic example of the believer who settles for worldly pleasure at the expense of eternal reward.

Let us rather emulate Moses who understood the importance and value of gaining eternal rewards and did everything to that end. *"He regarded disgrace for the sake of Christ as of greater value than the treasures of Egypt, because he was looking ahead to his reward"* (Hebrews 11:26). That should be our attitude. That should be the way we view life – from an eternal perspective. I challenge you to seriously think for a few moments about how you would fare at the Judgment Seat of Christ if you went there today. Do you think you would get a full reward or no reward? Think about your eternal destiny. Are you living in such a way as to win a prize on that day? If not, you had better make adjustments. You had better get your attitude in line with God's Word and run for the prize. You must be more determined than an Olympic runner training to win a gold medal. You must be more passionate than a businessman aiming to make his next profit. In other words no earthly pursuit should surpass your resolve to run for and win eternal rewards in heaven. It should be an active conscious pursuit. Don't settle for anything less. Set eternal goals and go after them.

Now, what exactly are these rewards and how do we qualify for them? Well, they include heavenly crowns, thrones, positions of authority, treasures and eternal responsibilities and privileges beyond our wildest imagination. There is no human language to adequately describe the glories that await the overcomer. God wants to qualify you for an eternal position in His kingdom. The position you occupy in eternity will be determined by your service here on earth. Think of it; you determine where you will sit in heaven. That should make you want to live your life differently.

You are either contributing to or subtracting from your eternal reward every day you live. So don't take this casually. Live for that day!

God wants to qualify you for an eternal position in His kingdom.

For Overcomers Only

> *"He who overcomes will inherit all this, and I will be His God and He will be my son"* (Revelation 21:7).

Rewards are only given to the saints who overcome. Many will make it to heaven, but not many may have been overcomers. So this section is written only for those who want nothing but the best of heaven. It is written for the saints who have resolved to live for the crowning day. If you read the seven letters to the seven churches you will notice a similar sentence in every one of them: "to him who overcomes." This implies that the promised rewards are only for overcomers. That is to say, if you are not living an overcoming life, you may enter heaven with absolutely no reward. The ticket to get to heaven comes by accepting Jesus as your Lord, but the rewards of eternity depend on your labour for the Kingdom while on earth. Your life on earth can only amount to something if it is lived for Him. Otherwise it will amount to a pile of ashes on that day.

God wants us to perform well and as a good Father He has made it possible for everyone to do well. He who does not want anyone to perish also does not want anyone to fail. Any child, any teenager, any adult or elderly person can live the life God requires provided they surrender to His grace. This grace is His enabling power to do God's will on earth. It will enable us to live holy (Titus 2:11-13) even as we look forward to seeing the Lord. So how do we access this grace? The Bible tells us that it's by faith (Ephesians 2:8). When we hear His word as we are hearing it now, we receive the grace to put it into practice when we accept it by faith in our hearts. Then when we begin to act in line with that word, the ability of God is right there to enable us fulfill it. This is an example of how faith in the grace of God makes us overcomers. God's grace makes us overcomers over temptation, tests, and trials that may come our way.

Now let me reiterate a thought I have expressed earlier: **rewards are given to overcomers only!** I want this thought to ring clear in your ears. I want it to haunt you in a good way. Let it motivate you to live for that day like a student studying to pass an important exam. If I can help you live this way, then my book will have achieved its purpose.

Are You Running For Eternal Crowns In Heaven?

Are you running for the crowns in heaven or you are running only for earthly prizes? Are you running to reach an eternal goal or you are pursuing only temporal ones? Are you living to impact eternity or you're living to make earthly history? Examine yourself and judge. Do you have an eternal perspective or do you have a temporal one? You be the judge.

Just imagine, the crowns are already there waiting for us to win them. They are waiting for someone to lay claim to them as surely as gold medals await the Olympic runners training for their day. Perhaps they are in a huge warehouse in Heaven. But the question is, who is going to wear them and consequently sit on the glorious thrones reserved only for overcomers and not commoners? Folks, this calls for urgent action. We must realign our lives to God's purpose and live each day as if it were our last. We must live as though Jesus is coming today. We must live rapture-ready!

Are You Aiming For A Glorious Throne?

The Bible speaks of places of honor in heaven. These places include thrones which crowned kings will occupy forever. They are the eternal positions promised to those who are victorious. They are reserved only for the overcomers in every age. These are offered to all and are the highest positions available to man. Not everyone will have a throne but only those who are overcomers in Him – who have actually lived an overcoming life here on earth. You could say they are practicing overcomers.

The Bible clearly shows us that the very throne of Christ is built in such a way that the glorious thrones of the overcomers will all be a part of His throne. Revelation 3:21 says, *"To Him who overcomes, I will give the right to sit with me on my throne, just as I overcame and sat down with my Father on His throne."* These thrones are so important that I want to stir up your heart to run for one. The Bible further states that those who will sit on these glorious thrones will be given authority to judge. The Apostle John declares this in Revelation 20:4 when He says, *"I saw thrones on which were seated those who had been given authority to judge."* That sounds like awesome responsibility to me! The life we now live is in preparation for the next. How well you live will determine your rank in the eternal kingdom.

Remember, those who humble themselves and serve faithfully in love like their Savior will sit with Him on His throne. What kind of honor is that? Indescribable! These glorious kings will be the highest ranking officials in the kingdom. They will be the envy of all creation, the elite of heaven. Does that mean that God loves them more than the lower ranked saints? No! He loves all men the same, however, these have followed Him much closer than others. They earned their place in His conquering train through love, humility and faithful service. They are the ones who receive God's best rewards and will eternally be closer to Him than the rest. Yet everyone will enjoy a blissful eternity but some more so than others.

Where Will You Sit In Eternity? (Reserved Seating for Overcomers Only)

John was not the only one to have seen the thrones in heaven. Daniel the prophet also had a revelation of the same. The scene depicted seems to be the judgment of the world. Here's what he saw:

> *"I kept looking until thrones were placed [for the assessors with the Judge], and the Ancient of Days [God, the eternal Father] took His seat, Whose garment was white as snow and the hair of His head like pure wool. His throne was like the fiery flame; its wheels were burning fire.*
>
> *A stream of fire came forth from before Him; a thousand thousands ministered to Him and ten thousand times ten thousand rose up and stood before Him; the Judge was seated [the court was in session] and the books were opened."* (Daniel 7:9-10 AMP).

The ones sitting on the thrones have a part to play on the great Day of Judgment. Here, the Amplified Bible refers to them as "assessors with the judge." These kings will be the main rulers under God in eternity. Will you be one of them? Or will you settle for just a small position in heaven. Like I mentioned earlier, Jesus said some will be called great in the kingdom and others will be called least. The choice is not up to God – it's up to you. Will you become the person who is worthy to sit with Him? If so, then let the Holy Spirit have His way. Let the Father's will be done in your life. Discover God's will and do it with all your heart all the while keeping your eyes on the prize. Live for that hope. Aim for that goal. *"Let your eyes look straight ahead, fix your gaze directly before you"* (Proverbs 4:25).

Don't forfeit this great prize of eternity like Esau lost his birthright. There's nothing worth losing this prize over. I pray that everyone reading this book will passionately pursue it with all their heart. You will determine where you sit in heaven by how you live today. How close you are to Him in this life will determine how close you will sit with Him in eternity. Those who will ride white horses closest to Him will be the ones who followed Him whole heartedly.

"To Him who overcomes, I will give the right to sit with me on my throne, just as I overcame and sat down with my Father on His throne" (Revelation 3:21). As for now, everyone has equal opportunity to run for this prize. It is open for all who will. The Bible is clear on how to do it: discover God's will and do it. This will require a humble heart and love for God and man. And when you faithfully serve Him, no doubt you will hear Him say, *"Well done, my good servant...Because you have been trustworthy in a very small matter, take charge of ten cities"* (Luke 19:17).

We must aim for a full reward. We must! These thrones are the greatest prizes you can ever run for in eternity. They are the apex of God's rewards. That is why when the Apostles asked the Lord what they would gain since they had forsaken all, He replied, *"I tell you the truth, at the renewal of all things, when the Son of Man sits on his glorious throne, you who have followed me will also sit on twelve thrones, judging the twelve tribes of Israel"* (Matthew 19:28). This was a promise given to the twelve apostles. But thank God there're more thrones besides the twelve and they are available for us to gain. Therefore *"...run in such a way as to get the prize"* (1 Corinthians 9:24b). We should always be *"looking unto Jesus the Author and Finisher of our faith"* (Hebrews 12:2).

I believe there'll be many more rewards that defy description - things that are impossible for the mind of man to imagine. All these are waiting to be won.

Your Heavenly Account

"Not because I desire a gift: but I desire fruit that may abound to your account" (Philippians 4:17).

This verse was written to a group of believers who were giving into Paul's ministry to help him minister and to supply his personal needs. They were the only church that communicated or shared with him in the matter of giving and receiving. He assured them that their earthly needs would be met and that also fruit would be credited to their account. That means that they would be blessed here on earth as a result of their financial support since the giver is more blessed than the receiver. But also their account in heaven would be credited with the good acts of service they had rendered. They would be partakers of Paul's grace here on earth as well as share in Paul's reward at the Judgment Seat of Christ. This is why it is important to support soul-winning ministries. The reward for soul-winning they get will also be credited to your account.

Jesus put it this way: *"I tell you, use worldly wealth to gain friends for yourselves, so that when it is gone, you will be welcomed into eternal dwellings"* (Luke 16:9). This is one of the wisest uses of wealth recorded in scripture. The greatest investment you can make is to help a soul get to heaven. Jesus admonishes us to use our money and possessions to gain something that will far outlast them. He wants us to invest in souls – the most precious thing in God's creation. We must partner with soul-winning ministries and pour our money into evangelistic crusades, church outreaches and production of evangelistic materials. The result will be that we will be received or welcomed by many souls in heaven that we helped win to the Lord. They will be the everlasting joy of our lives – our eternal crown.

So don't let your heavenly account be empty. Make deposits regularly by doing good to all – giving to the poor, paying tithes and offerings to your local church, supporting the gospel, etc. Then when you get to heaven you will be amazed at how your giving, small as it may have seemed, accumulated into a great heavenly reward. Your accomplishments on earth may not seem so significant to you, but if done sincerely as unto the Lord they will count for much. The important thing is to give according to your ability with a heart to bless others. Don't be selfish. The bible in 1Timothy 6:17-19 further admonishes us to invest in what lasts.

> *"Command those who are rich in this present world not to be arrogant nor to put their hope in wealth, which is so uncertain, but to put their hope in God, who richly provides us with everything for our enjoyment.*
>
> *Command them to do good, to be rich in good deeds, and to be generous and willing to share.*
>
> *In this way they will lay up treasure for themselves as a firm foundation for the coming age, so that they may take hold of the life that is truly life."*

Every kingdom businessman or rich person needs to take heed to this scripture. Greed and selfishness have to go. You reap what you sow. Your financial investments in the kingdom are not in vain. They will be richly rewarded.

Gaining Eternal Rewards

One of the greatest ways to obtain eternal rewards is to love those that may never love you back and be good to those that may never return the favor. Some time back while pondering just how I could live in such a way as to obtain maximum rewards, I heard these words in my heart: "He who loves the most will be rewarded the most." Those words are etched on my memory and I want nothing less than that in eternity. I want to qualify for the best that God has on offer!

Now if love has something to do with gaining eternal rewards then I want to know all about it. Nothing we do in this life will have eternal value without love. If the motive is not love then it will be counted as nothing. Nothing you do will profit you unless it is done out of the motive of love. Now let's delve into the word of God to see what kind of love we are talking about.

Jesus said, *"If you love only those who love you, what reward will you get? Are not even the tax collectors doing that?"* (Matthew 5:46). So in order to obtain love's reward you'll have to love more than just your friends and loved ones. You need to spread your wings to the orphan, the widow, the stranger, the homeless, the sick, the poor, the prisoners, the disabled and the rejected. Your love must extend to those who are not even considered loveable. That is the love that God will honor.

"And if you greet only your brothers, what are you doing more than others? Do not even the pagans do that?" (Matthew 5:47). We need to go the extra mile my friends. We need to get out of our comfort zones and love the unlovable. Yes, we even need to be kind to the ungrateful. It's not about who is going to love us back or return the favor. It's about loving the way God loves – sacrificially and unconditionally. Knowing we'll be rewarded in heaven, we can gladly love our enemies, bless those who curse us, do good to those who hate us, and pray for those who abuse and persecute us (Matthew 5:44).

This would all be unbearable if it wasn't for the love of God shed abroad in our hearts. It would not be possible to love such people if it wasn't for the fact that God's unconditional love dwells in us. But what is even more exciting is that for every person we love there is added value to our rewards in heaven.

That's what makes it all worthwhile. So you are not showing kindness to your enemy in vain (even if she's your mother-in-law). The rewards for loving such people are immense.

> *"But love your enemies, do good to them, and lend to them without expecting to get anything back. Then your reward will be great, and you will be sons of the Most High, because he is kind to the ungrateful and wicked. Be merciful, just as your Father is merciful"* (Luke 6:35-36).

So you see that heavenly rewards are to a large degree based on how you treat other people. It's not what people do to you but how you respond to them that matters. Overcome evil with good. It doesn't matter whether it's at work, at home or school, you need to walk in love just the same. Don't worry about who hates you. You just keep showing them God's love anyway.

One of the most awesome scriptures in the bible is found in James 1:27: *"Religion that God our Father accepts as pure and faultless is this: to look after orphans and widows in their distress and to keep oneself from being polluted by the world."* That's true Christianity!

It is amazing that the things that could make us kings in heaven are simple and often overlooked. They are lowly and don't require you to be a great intellectual to do them. They are attainable for anyone that has a willing heart.

Jesus said that *"...when you give a banquet, invite the poor, the crippled, the lame, the blind and you will be blessed"* (Luke 14:12). Have you ever thought of throwing a party for the underprivileged in society? Although they cannot repay you, you will be repaid when the Lord comes. Yes, you will also reap benefits in this life! *"Blessed is he that considereth the poor: the Lord will deliver him in time of trouble. The Lord will preserve him, and keep him alive; and he shall be blessed upon the earth: and thou wilt not deliver him unto the will of his enemies. The*

Lord will strengthen him upon the bed of languishing: thou wilt make all his bed in his sickness" (Psalm 41:1-3 KJV).

Someone needs to reach down to the rejects and outcasts and pull them up to experience love. Someone needs to go to the prisons and give gifts and minister God's love to the prisoners. Someone needs to make the lives of the homeless more bearable. But who will, if not you and me? We all need to do something about it.

Losing Eternal Rewards

Knowing how to gain rewards is important. But we must also learn how rewards are lost so that we can take precautions.

Like I said before, every day that you live, you are either gaining or losing rewards. The word of God not only tells us how to gain rewards but also how losses occur. The subject of losses is not a very pleasant one but it is a necessary one to learn. We need to know the things that can disqualify us so that we can avoid them.

So in the next few pages I want us to look at a few of those things and see how we can avoid them in our lives.

1.   Do Nothing

The surest way to not gain rewards is to do nothing for God. The Bible tells us that if we know how to do good but do not do it, then to us it is a sin. This is what has come to be known as the sin of omission. It's a sin of negligence and irresponsibility. You know what you are supposed to do but you don't do it.

God will hold us accountable for not applying what we know. He will call us to account for wasted opportunities and neglected duty. A lot of us know quite a lot of things. We know how to pray, and we can evangelize. We know about giving to the poor and we know what God has said about how we should treat our enemies. We also know how that we should do everything as unto the Lord. Yet many times we are negligent. Now, we may not be committing an act of unrighteousness but we are omitting an act of righteousness. And that does amount to unrighteousness.

The wicked and lazy servant in the parable of the talents did not do anything profitable with his money but hid it in the ground while others made theirs productive. The Master had no kind words for this lazy servant. He rebuked him and assigned him a very low place in keeping with his poor results. This is why he's weeping and gnashing his teeth. He's in the lowest place in heaven. However heaven will still be a blissful experience for him even without a reward. But it could have been better. Never neglect your talent but use it to the full. So if you're not using what you have, you have a case to answer.

Therefore, to have biblical knowledge and not use it is to sin. To have ability and not use it is to be a liability to the kingdom. The bible is very clear that those who do nothing will gain nothing. In fact even the reward they were supposed to get will go to someone else. That's why Jesus warns you and I in Revelation 3:11 *"...Hold on to what you have, so that no one will take your crown."*

Let's make every effort to be diligent with what we know. We must put into practice God's word and make every effort to use our talents, gifts and abilities for Him. Then we can expect to hear Him say, "Well done!" We must take one opportunity at a time and use it to the fullest. Let us be faithful and diligent that we may not suffer loss on that day. We are to be diligent not negligent!

> *"Behold, I am coming soon! My reward is with me, and I will give to everyone according to what he has done"* (Revelation 22:12).

Jesus is coming to reward us according to what we have done, not according to what we have not done. The reaping of rewards is not a hit and miss game. It is a direct result of the seeds of faithful service that you sow in this life. Every act of obedience goes to increase your harvest in heaven. So don't just stand there, do something! Do the works that God created you to do.

2.   Do Something with the Wrong Motives

Every good deed done with wrong motives will be judged as worthless in the sight of God. Even prayer done to impress men will be counted as worthless at the Judgment Seat of Christ. The Bible says, *"When you pray, do not be like the hypocrites, for they love to pray standing in the synagogues and on the street corners to be seen by men. I tell you the truth they have received their reward in full"* (Matthew 6:5).That means no heavenly reward for them. In fact the only earthly reward they get is the admiration of men. God will not even answer such prayer much less reward it!

On the other hand, we are supposed to pray in private or if we do pray in public, it should be with the right motive to address God and not to impress men.

Our giving also must be practiced in such a way as not to seek the honor of men but to be a blessing like God wants us to be. *"Be careful not to do your acts of righteousness before men, to be seen by them. If you do, you will have no reward from your Father in heaven"* (Matthew 6:1). Your motives in giving must be pure if you expect to get a reward. Giving to impress people is as bad as greed or covetousness. But the Lord honors a cheerful giver – both now and forevermore.

It blesses me to just think of Cornelius – a man who prayed and gave much to the needy. He was commended by God and attracted God's attention. The bible says *"...he gave generously to those in need and prayed to God regularly"* (Acts 10:2b). Then an angel appeared to him and said to him, *"...your prayers and gifts to the poor have come up as a memorial offering before God"* (Acts 10:4b).

So whether it's praying, giving, fasting or whatever else we do, let us do it heartily as unto the Lord, not unto men. It will save us unnecessary losses at the Judgment Seat of Christ.

3.   Do the Wrong Thing Altogether

Now God forgives our personal moral sins but we will have to give account for some wrong actions that had negative consequences for the kingdom. For example, if you did something that caused someone else to lose confidence in Christ, you will be held responsible for the state that person fell into. We can't put stumbling blocks in other people's paths and expect to get away with it. Jesus said that *"It is impossible but that offences will come: but woe unto him, through whom they come. It were better for him that a millstone were hanged about his neck, and he cast in the sea, than that he should offend one of these little ones"* (Luke 17:1-2 KJV). There is definitely no reward for doing things that cause other people to stumble. If we make people stumble we are demoting only ourselves. We are cutting away from our eternal reward in Christ. Some of the consequences of our negative actions are far greater than we realize. King Saul lost an opportunity far more than meets the eye. His disobedience to God's command cost him the opportunity to be king of Israel forever. The Bible is clear that David who replaced Saul and followed God closely will be given the position of king of Israel as his eternal reward with the twelve apostles of the Lamb ruling under him (Ezekiel 37:24-28;Matthew 19:28).This is what Saul could have had, but he blew it. You can't just live without fulfilling God's will and expect to get a throne in heaven. The consequences of disobedience to God's call are costly.

You can't ruin someone else's reputation to further your own. If you get into leadership by stepping on other people's toes, you had better watch out! There's a day of reckoning coming. What will you say to Him on that day? It's time to clean up our act, saints. Succeeding at the expense of others is failure in God's eyes. If you rise by putting others down, then your fall will be great and your position in heaven low. Those who exalt themselves shall be humbled but those who humble themselves will be exalted. Watch how you treat people and be careful to lift them up when they are down. By so doing you are sowing the seeds of promotion in your life. Create a platform for others to succeed. Their success will be credited to you as well. There's no use trying to suppress others. Keeping other people down simply because you are insecure or jealous will work against you on that day. But promoting other people to advance God's cause will bring you rewards beyond your imagination. *"And whatever you do, whether in word or deed, do all, in the name of the Lord Jesus, giving thanks to God the Father through Him"* (Colossians 3:17).

Five Eternal Crowns

Now let's take a look at the eternal rewards and how to run to win them. We will concentrate on the five crowns mentioned in scripture. They are:

1. The Victor's Crown
2. The Soul Winner's Crown
3. The Crown of Righteousness
4. The Crown of Life
5. The Crown of Glory

We can now look at each one of these in detail.

1.   The Victor's Crown

> *"Similarly, if anyone competes as an athlete, he does not receive the victor's crown unless he competes according to the rules"* (2 Timothy 2:5).

74

"Do you not know that in a race all the runners run, but only one gets the prize? Everyone who competes in the games goes into strict training. They do it to get a crown that will not last; but we do it to get a crown that will last forever. Therefore I do not run like a man running aimlessly; I do not fight like a man beating the air. No, I beat my body and make it my slave so that after I have preached to others, I myself will not be disqualified for the prize" (1 Corinthians 9: 24-27).

Also known as the Imperishable or Incorruptible Crown, this crown is given to the Christian who runs his spiritual race with perseverance, dedication, diligence, determination and discipline. It is awarded to those who live a sacrificial life by denying their fleshly desires to fulfill God's will. They *"Do nothing out of selfish ambition or vain conceit, but in humility consider others better than [themselves]"* (Philippians 2:3). They sacrifice their own desires to be a blessing to others. They discipline their body so that they can be effective in their spiritual walk. They carry their cross daily and keep their body in subjection to their spirit. They put to death the deeds of the flesh. Those who fail to discipline the flesh will be disqualified for the prize.

This crown might as well be called the Runner's Crown because the first analogy given is that of a runner and in athletics disciplined training is the key to success. No one ever won an Olympic Gold Medal without strict training. It takes a lot of discipline to train, practice and follow a strict diet. But the athlete does this for a perishable medal while we discipline our flesh for a crown that will last forever! Without discipline you cannot win an Olympic Medal much less a heavenly crown. Crowns are for overcomers and you have to overcome to win this crown. Crowns are won. They are not given as gifts. No wonder the Bible tells us to *"...throw off everything that hinders and the sin that so easily entangles, and let us run with perseverance the race marked out for us"* (Hebrews 12:1b).

Application

What are some of the ways you can increase your chances of winning this crown?

- Removing weights or things that hinder your spiritual life. Some of these could be wrong friendships that weigh you down spiritually.
- Dealing with besetting sins that easily cause you to stumble spiritually. You do that by abiding in the word and trusting God's grace to abound to you.
- Ensuring that you crucify the flesh with its passions and appetites. You do this through prayer and making selfless choices in love.
- Being more determined than an Olympic runner in your spiritual race. Make a quality decision to put eternal rewards on your goal setting program. Eternal goals are more important than temporal ones. There's a great cloud of witnesses cheering for you from heaven. Let them inspire you to run to the finish line with joy, fixing your eyes on Jesus the author and finisher of our faith. So run to finish your race and win the prize.

2.   The Soul Winner's Crown

As the name suggests, this crown is awarded to the faithful soul winner who spent his life bringing the lost to Christ. He is a savior of men on behalf of His King. He takes the time to preach the gospel to those who live in darkness. He is on a rescue mission for heaven. He does it for the love of God, the love of souls and the crown in heaven.

> *"For what is our hope, our joy, or the crown in which we will glory in the presence of our Lord Jesus when He comes? Indeed, you are our glory and joy"* (1 Thessalonians 2:19-20)

One of the greatest joys of being in heaven will be to see the souls that you brought to the Lord while on earth. This ought to motivate all of us to go out and win the lost and make disciples of them. Why? We ourselves would probably be lost if someone didn't preach to us. Not only that, we are called to be witnesses of Christ to a lost and dying world.

The measure of glory and joy that you will experience in heaven is in relation to your works on earth. And one such work is soul winning. The bible says that, *"Those who are wise will shine like the brightness of the heavens, and those who lead many to righteousness like the stars forever and ever"* (Daniel 12:3). That's the glory of soul winners.

We need to use every resource we have – time, money, ability – to reach out so we can bring the lost to Christ. Let us endeavor to use every effort to win them more so as we see the day approaching. Our mandate has still not changed. We must *"...Go into all the world and preach the good news to all creation"* (Mark 16:15) *"...go and make disciples of all nations..."* (Matthew 28:19). We must get our relatives saved. We must see to it that our neighbors, workmates and school mates accept the Lord. We must get as many people to heaven as possible. Let us do it knowing that one day we will receive an eternal crown of rejoicing. My dear friend, do all you can to learn about soul winning and get busy harvesting. If you are very timid and lazy, find someone who is a good soul winner and let them teach you how. Let your giving be directed to soul winning ventures. Sooner or later you will be passionate about the lost and great will be your reward!

3.   The Crown of Righteousness

> *"I have fought the good fight, I have finished the race, I have kept the faith. Now there is in store for me the crown of righteousness, which the Lord, the righteous judge, will award to me on that day – and not only to me, but also to all who have longed for his appearing"* (2 Timothy 4:7-8).

This crown is reserved for those who have been victorious as good boxers in the fight of faith, run as disciplined athletes with perseverance and finished their spiritual course, and have kept their loyalty of faith to Him without wavering. These all-weather Christians who also long for His appearing will qualify for this special crown.

You could call it a crown for those who live in the light of His return. They are actively anticipating His appearance and so they work and live their lives as though He could come at any moment. They live rapture-ready, keeping their lamps burning for Him! Indeed the hope of His return inspires them to serve Him more diligently. It helps them live more holy so that they conduct their affairs with discretion knowing any moment the trumpet might blow. *"Dear friends, now we are children of God, and what we will be has not yet been made known. But we know that when He appears, we shall be like Him, for we shall see Him as He is. Everyone who has this hope in Him purifies himself, just as He is pure"* (1 John 3:2-3).

These ready-to-go believers will be awarded a special crown for their longing to be with Him. That's why I consider the coming of Jesus a very vital doctrine. It even has a special crown associated with it. This should be our living hope - our blessed hope. We are not running away from responsibility when we focus on Christ's return. In fact we are being more responsible by preparing ourselves to meet Him at His coming. We want to be about our Father's business till Christ comes. We want to make the most of every opportunity. Our priorities must be in order. Time is running out. We want to be presented a radiant church without spot or wrinkle or any other blemish (Ephesians 5:27).

4.   The Crown of Life

"Blessed is the man who perseveres under trial, because when he has stood the test, he will receive the crown of life that God has promised to those who love Him" (James 1:12)

Also known as the Martyr's Crown, this crown is given to those who overcome tests and trials and love the Lord. They have proven their love for Him in spite of temptations and trials. They have passed the loyalty test and are worthy to receive this great honor. They are those who overcame Satan by the blood of the Lamb and the word of their testimony and loved not their lives unto the death (Revelation 12:11). They laid down their lives for the Master in sacrificial service unto Him. They endured persecution and stood fast without denying Him. They shared in His sufferings and so they'll share in His glory. They were never ashamed of the gospel before men. They never disowned Him before men. They were never ashamed to be called Christians but stood as witnesses of the Light.

This crown is promised to those who love Him. It only makes sense that the greatest commandment has a special crown attached to it. It is quite clear that if you love the Lord you will also love men who are created in His image. To not love men is to not love God. *"If anyone says, I love God, yet hates his brother, he is a liar. For anyone who does not love his brother, whom he has seen, cannot love God, whom he has not seen. And He has given us this command: Whoever loves God must also love his brother"* (1 John 4:20-21). This is the crown given for loving the Lord more than yourself or anybody else for that matter. It is for those who emulate the love that Jesus demonstrated by laying down His life for His friends. We too can lay down our lives for others in loving service unto the Lord. *"...Be faithful, even to the point of death, and I will give you the crown of life"* (Revelation 2:10b). It is given to those who die as martyrs (killed in His name) and those who live as martyrs every day of their lives, laying down their lives for the sake of others. You can't afford to miss it. Go for the crown!

It is important to distinguish between the crown of life which is a reward for service, and eternal life which is a gift of grace. The crown of life will not be given to every believer. It will only be given to those who fulfilled the conditions for receiving it. The gift of eternal life on the other hand is given to every believer right here on earth when Jesus comes into our hearts. Eternal life is a possession of every believer right now and forever. Eternal life is not simply a state of endless existence. It is actually the life of God inside of us. It is His nature of love, righteousness and holiness in us. This divine nature of eternal life is in every believer right now. But the crown of life is a reward reserved for those who qualify for it, and will be given to then on that day.

5.   The Crown of Glory

"Be shepherds of God's flock that is under your care, serving as overseers – not because you must, but because you are willing, as God wants you to be; not greedy for money, but eager to serve; not lording it over those entrusted to you, but being examples to the flock. And when the Chief Shepherd appears, you will receive the crown of glory that will never fade away" (1 Peter 5:2-4).

This crown is promised to the faithful leaders of God's flock. It is a reward for those who take care of God's people by feeding them spiritually and nurturing them to maturity in Christ. These are pastors, teachers, cell leaders, fellowship leaders, Sunday school teachers or anybody else who ministers to a group of people on a regular basis.

You remember that Jesus gave Peter three commands concerning His flock. I used to think that Jesus said the same thing three times but the Lord helped me see that they were three distinct commands.

1.   **Feed my lambs** – This means baby Christians who should be fed the sincere milk of the word that they may grow thereby. They must be grounded in the fundamentals of the Christian faith as outlined in Hebrews 6:1-3.
2.   **Take care of my sheep** – This means to guard and protect the flock as a whole. See to it that the wolves that may divide the flock are kept away. Be a

shepherd like the Good Shepherd who lays down his life for the sheep and leaves the 99 to go after the 1. Never be willing to let a single sheep stray. In this command He also meant for the shepherd to care for or counsel the hurting and injured sheep binding up their wounds.

3. **Feed my sheep** – This is a command to feed the mature saints with the strong meat of God's word so that they can take responsibility in the body of Christ. They need more than spiritual milk. They must be fed to adequately match their task in life. They can't survive on one cold spiritual snack a week. They must eat hot spiritual food regularly. We must watch what we teach because God will hold us accountable for our teachings and the results they produce. James actually says that those who teach will be judged more strictly because teaching has the potential to do the worst imaginable damage or greatest good for the body of Christ (James 3:1). Wrong teaching can even lead people astray, while sound doctrine can make the saints sound or healthy in their faith. Remember, scriptural teaching is the primary way to produce disciples who are just like Christ. *"Therefore go and make disciples of all nations...teaching them to obey everything I have commanded you ..."* (Matthew 28:19-20). The primary way to make disciples who are like Christ is to teach them what Christ taught as outlined in the Gospels and to build on from there.

This work of maturing people into Christ-likeness carries a special reward. But don't feel left out, because the bible says that He who receives a prophet in the name of a prophet will get a prophet's reward (Matthew 10:41). That means they'll be blessed in this life and they'll also share in the eternal reward of the prophet (leader). So it goes without saying that those who faithfully support the leader of God's flock with prayers, time and material resources shall also be entitled to this glorious crown on that day. That ought to make you shout! That is why it's so important to honor your spiritual leaders. The person who leads God's people must not do it out of mere duty but must be willing to do so serving joyfully from the heart and being a good example to the flock.

Privileges for Overcomers

- Overcomers will have the right to eat from the tree of life (Revelation 2:7).
- Overcomers will not be hurt by the second death (Revelation 2:11).
- Overcomers will be given some of the hidden manna, and a white stone with a new private name inscribed on it, pretty much like a password (Revelation 2:17).
- Overcomers who do God's will to the end will be given authority over the nations and will also receive the morning star (Revelation 2:26-28).
- Overcomers will be dressed in white and will never be blotted out of the book of life but will be honored before the Father and His angels. Who will be Master of Ceremony? Jesus Himself (Revelation 3:5).
- Overcomers will be made permanent pillars in the temple of God and will have inscribed on their foreheads the name of God, the name of the heavenly city and the name of the Son as a very special honor (Revelation 3:12).
- Now this is a big one. I consider it the greatest honor. Overcomers will be given the right to sit with Christ on His throne just as He overcame and sat down with the Father on His throne. These overcomers will be the highest ranking officials of God's kingdom forever (Revelation 3:21). They are the ones referred to in Revelation 22:5b: *"...and they shall reign forever and ever."*

I believe some of these privileges belong to every saint who will be in heaven by virtue of 1 John 5:4 which says, *"for everyone born of God overcomes the world. This is the victory that has overcome the world, even our faith. Who is it that overcomes the world? Only he who believes that Jesus is the Son of God"* (1 John 5:4-5). But privileges such as ruling over the nations and sitting on Christ's throne are only for those who lived an overcoming life apart from their initial victory in the new birth. You see, certain aspects of eternity will be enjoyed equally but there will be many privileges and responsibilities only given to the practicing overcomers. This is the reason we must live in victory over the flesh, the world, and the devil. The lust of the flesh, the lust of the eyes, and the pride of life must all be subdued. There's a reward for living the more-than-conquerors life.

Just think of yourself as a spiritual war veteran returning from the battle field to a rousing welcome by the great cloud of witnesses. You have fought a good fight, you have finished your race, and have kept the faith. You have sacrificed for others and have rescued many from the enemy's camp. You have been a disciplined soldier enduring hardship for the name of Christ. Now you come face to face with your Commander who is more than pleased to welcome you home with great honors. Your ranking goes up and many medals grace your new uniform. You are appointed to a much higher position than you ever dreamed of. This day of your great honor has come and it makes all of those gruesome battles on earth worthwhile. It makes all of the sacrifice and pain look small. You have made it to heaven a champion, a winner in God's eyes. Receive your reward and enjoy it. That's what each of us should long for in Christ. The apostle Peter puts it this way: *"Therefore, my brothers, be all the more eager to make your calling and election sure. For if you do these things, you will never fall, and you will receive a rich welcome into the eternal kingdom of our Lord and Savior Jesus Christ"* (2 Peter 1:10-11). That means it is possible that some will not receive a rousing welcome in heaven. Saints, let us do everything we can so that we may not be ashamed at His appearing. Let us live the life of love and overcome by faith in Him as we go about fulfilling His will and not ours.

CHAPTER 4

TWO ETERNAL DESTINIES

Where do you want to spend eternity? Where do you want to go when this life is over? There can only be one of two places – heaven or hell. We can't live life pretending there is no heaven or hell because there is. The Bible is very clear that hell is a real place that exists beneath the surface of the earth in what is known as the underworld. It is a place of such severe torment there is nothing to compare it with on earth. It is the prison of rebellious souls held until the great Judgment of the White Throne. It is a most dreadful place to go to and no one in their right mind ought to want to go there. The bible tells us that the fires of hell torment souls night and day with no opportunity for rest. It is the most horrible place imaginable second only to the lake of fire which is the final abode of the wicked. This place was not created for mankind in the first place. But the sad part is that people who follow the devil will end up there with him. This is the fate of every sinner who won't repent.

But the good news is that as much as hell is a totally horrible place, heaven by contrast is an immensely glorious place. It is the most perfectly beautiful place you can ever imagine. It has streets of pure gold and walls made out of precious stones. It is so extraordinarily beautiful that human language can hardly begin to describe it. It is the hope of all the saints and a place of the greatest pleasure and joy that can ever be experienced. It is the place of righteous souls who commit their lives to the Lord by accepting Him into their hearts. No one can ever get there except those who have been washed in the blood of the Lamb. Are you going to be there? The choice is yours. Take the time to reflect on your life and see if you are right with God. Make sure you know your status to avoid going to a place you were never meant to go. Trust in the Lord and let Him save you from your sins. Repent and believe the good news that Jesus died to save your soul from sin and eternal doom. Call upon Him now and accept Him as your Lord. You cannot take chances with this one. Your eternal welfare is at stake. Or perhaps you are a backslidden soul. I beg you, my dear friend, to swallow your pride and forget your shame. God still loves you and He wants to heal your backslidings. Take a bold step and repent calling upon the name of the Lord to restore you. Why should you go to hell when you know the truth? Go to heaven instead. That's where you're meant to be.

The following table contrasts the horrors of hell with the glories of heaven. (Please note that this is not a complete listing of the differences between these two places).

HORRORS OF HELL	GLORIES OF HEAVEN
The Curse	The Blessing
Pain and Torment	Pleasure and Rest
Suffering	Joy
Gross Darkness	Great Light
Weeping	Laughter
Shame	Glory
Condemnation	Freedom
Loneliness	Fellowship
Separation From God	The Presence of God
Demons	Angels
Punishment	Rewards
Defeat	Victory
Regret	Consolation
Humiliation	Exaltation

The World Beneath

There are three worlds revealed in scripture.

1. **Heaven** (where God, the holy angels and departed saints live)

2.   **Earth** (this is where we are right now).
3.   **The Underworld** (that is the region of the damned inside the earth).

The bible says in Philippians 2:11 *"that at the name of Jesus every knee should bow, in heaven and on earth and under the earth."* Other translations actually say *"beings in heaven, beings on earth and beings under the earth."* The middle or transitory world is the earth from where you determine where you will go after this life is over. Heaven is the world far above this one and will one day become one with the renewed earth as the eternal home of righteousness. The underworld, where fallen beings will forever be consigned, is also a real world somewhere inside this earth. It is this world below I want us to look at in detail.

I want us to see what the scripture actually teaches about this dark region of the damned. The Bible shows us that before Jesus' death, resurrection and ascension, the underworld was composed of five compartments namely,

- Tarturus,
- Hades or Hell,
- The Abyss or Bottomless Pit,
- The Lake of Fire, and
- Abraham's Bosom or Paradise.

Now let's look at these departments one by one.

1.   Tarturus

"For if God did not spare angels when they sinned, but sent them to hell, putting them into gloomy dungeons to be held for judgment" (2 Peter 2:4).

The footnote of my NIV bible says that the Greek word translated Hell in this verse is Tarturus. In the Greek language it is clear that this place is not the same region where the souls of wicked men go to when they die. Rather, Tarturus is the prison of angels who sinned most probably during Noah's time when they mated with the daughters of men thus producing a race of giants who were half-man-half-angel.

These fallen angels are currently chained in Tarturus until the day of judgment. It would be good for us to establish this fact by looking at what Jude says in his book. *"And the angels who did not keep their positions of authority but abandoned their own home – these he has kept in darkness, bound with everlasting chains for judgment on the Great Day"* (Jude 6). So we see that this special group of angels is not freely roaming the earth or doing anything in the underworld. They are bound with everlasting chains until that awesome Day.

Now concerning the judgment of these fallen angels, who do you suppose will judge them? Is it Jesus? I don't suppose so. The bible, if allowed to speak for itself, tells us that the glorified saints will judge the fallen angels and assist Jesus in His final judgment of sinful men. *"Do you not know that the saints will judge the world? And if you are to judge the world, are you not competent to judge trivial cases? Do you not know that we will judge angels? How much more the things of this life!"* (1 Corinthians 6:2-3). It is an awesome responsibility, when you seriously think about it.

God is holy and just. He never has, does not and never will tolerate sin in His presence. He hates wickedness and loves righteousness. He expects us to take heed to ourselves lest we end up being condemned with the devil and his evil angels. Has He not shown us mercy and grace by creating a way of escape for us through accepting His Son Jesus? *"Let no one deceive you with empty words, for because of such things God's wrath comes on those who are disobedient. Therefore do not be partakers with them"* (Ephesians 5:6-7). Ignoring this warning could lead to the deepest regret imaginable.

2.   Hades

Hades is the Greek word translated hell in many instances including the Luke 16 account about the rich man and Lazarus.

In verse 23 Jesus reveals the fact that the stingy rich man went to a place called Hades when he died. This and not Tarturus is the place of fiery torment where the wicked go at the time of their death. Here they await the day when Jesus will resurrect all the wicked who have died since the time of Adam. *"Just as a man is destined to die once, and after that to face judgment"* (Hebrews 9:27).

So when we say sinners who die go to hell, it means they go to this place of torment which in the Greek language is called Hades. It is one of the departments of the underworld and the Lord does not want anyone to go there. He is not willing that any should perish. The Lord does not delight in the death of the wicked. He delights in their repentance towards Him. He has even delayed His coming for that very reason.

Now, I don't know anyone in their right mind who after hearing about hell would want to go there and be subjected to the most fearsome of all judgments.

3.   **The Abyss or Bottomless Pit**

The Abyss or Bottomless Pit is another separate region of the underworld where Satan will one day be imprisoned for a thousand years. This will be in order to keep him from deceiving the nations during the millennial reign of Christ. Then at the end of the one thousand years he will be released for a season to test those born during the millennial reign so they too can choose their own eternal destiny.

The Bottomless Pit is at this present time occupied by evil spirits who in the near future will be released to wreck havoc in the earth. How do I know this? Revelation 9:1-11 says so. The evil spirits who are there now will be released during the great tribulation to torment men and women to such a point that people will seek death but will not find it. We don't know all there is to know about the Abyss but one thing is for sure: it is a different compartment of the underworld for a different purpose. There is no mention of human souls being consigned there.

4.   The Lake of Fire

The lake of fire is the final and eternal place of punishment where every enemy of God both human and non-human will spend eternity. It is not a place that any one of us should go to, but unfortunately multitudes will wind up there because they never took the way of escape that was available to them.

The first people who will be cast into that fiery lake will be the Antichrist and the False Prophet following their defeat at Armageddon when Jesus Christ returns. The next personality to join them will be Satan at the end of the millennial reign of Christ right after leading his final rebellion against God. Then after that comes the Great White Throne Judgment at which anyone whose name is not found written in the Lamb's Book of Life will be cast into that fiery lake to writhe in pain forever and ever. To be tormented with burning sulfur is something we must avoid at all costs. *"But the cowardly, the unbelieving, the vile, the murderers, the sexually immoral, those who practice magic arts, the idolaters and all liars – their place will be in the fiery lake of burning sulphur. This is the second death"* (Revelation 21:8). I pray that this does not have to be you. Repent or else it may be too late.

5.   Abraham's Bosom or Paradise

In the beginning God created a special place called the Garden of Eden for
 man to enjoy. Not all the earth was a paradise so it was man's responsibility to duplicate that beautiful garden all over the earth. But unfortunately man rebelled against God and had to be banished from the garden. However God had a plan to restore man. So He set it into motion immediately by announcing it to him and introducing blood sacrifices until the day of the final sacrifice.

The paradise that man had on earth was no longer available or even accessible to him. God however made a special place of rest inside the earth called Abraham's Bosom where the souls of righteous men who died could be at rest until the Redeemer came to pay the price for man's sin. So from the time since Adam fell until the crucifixion, all righteous souls went to this temporary resting place at death. How do we know this? Jesus, in the true story of the rich man and Lazarus, makes it clear for us. In that story the rich man was able to see and communicate with Abraham because Hades, where the rich man was in torment, was located next to Abraham's Bosom with a huge gap or chasm separating the two places. In Abraham's reply to the rich man's request for water he said, *"And besides all this, between us and you there is a great gulf fixed, so that they which would pass from hence to you cannot, neither can they pass to us, that would come from thence"* (Luke 16:26 KJV).

The Bible doesn't say much about this place, but we know from what Jesus revealed that it was a place of comfort where even water was available (Luke 16:25). But thank God the day came when Jesus took everyone out of that temporary resting place and took them to their eternal home in heaven. In fact Matthew 27:50-52 tells us that those people were resurrected at the time of Jesus' death and resurrection. It says, *"And when Jesus had cried out again in a loud voice, he gave up his spirit. At that moment the curtain of the temple was torn from top to bottom. The earth shook and the rocks split. The tombs broke open and the bodies of many holy people who had died were raised to life. They came out of the tombs, and after Jesus' resurrection they went into the holy city and appeared to many people."*

Ephesians 4:8-10 sheds a bit more light on what actually happened after Jesus rose from the dead. It is also clear from this passage that Jesus took those saints with Him to heaven. *"This is why it says: When he ascended on high, he led captives in his train and gave gifts to men. (What does "he ascended" mean except that he also descended to the lower, earthly regions? He who descended is the very one who ascended higher than all the heavens, in order to fill the whole universe.)"*

So from the time Jesus paid the price for man's sin, the souls of righteous people who die now ascend to heaven to be with the Lord. Even when Jesus will descend from heaven to take the prepared saints out of this world so they don't go through the tribulation, it's in heaven where they'll be until He returns with them seven years later to set up His one thousand year rule here on earth.

Avoiding the Worst of Dooms

Some will say, "We shouldn't scare people into the kingdom. Let's just tell them about the love of God." Well, I'm not for scaring people into the kingdom, but I'm for warning people about the dangers of sin and the coming judgment. In fact the true love of God warns people about what would hurt them. Those you truly love, you will warn not to go down a certain road. It is my responsibility to warn you in love that if you don't repent and believe on the Lord Jesus Christ then you're headed for the worst of dooms. I cannot sugar-coat this message to make it more widely acceptable. It must be told as it is. I would rather make you tremble with this message than pamper you on your way to eternal fire.

The Bible describes the final abode of the wicked as a fiery lake of burning sulphur where the smoke of their torment rises forever and ever. It is no joke my friends. There are people in Hell right now being tormented as they await the final judgment when they will be cast into the eternal lake of fire. The Bible calls it the second death. It is far worse than you could ever imagine. The intense pain, regret, agony and shame can hardly be described.

The burning sulfur can be likened to the larva that pours out of an active volcano or the hot liquid metal from a fiery furnace. Now just imagine being thrown into a liquid like that and you haven't even begun to describe the lake of fire. Why should you be like those in hell crying out, "Why, Oh why, did I not repent? Why did I waste that opportunity?" Oh friends, that should not be you. That should not be how you end up.

Like I've already said, personally I don't know anyone in their right mind who would want to go there. I don't see why anyone would want to follow Satan to that place of eternal punishment. It was never designed for men but for the devil and his angels. They are the ones who belong there. But unfortunately there are people who will follow Satan all the way to eternal damnation. What a waste! They could have enjoyed eternity with God but chose otherwise.

Now the devil is well aware that his doom is already spelled out so he's doing all he can to take as many people with him as possible. *"But woe to the earth and the sea, because the devil has gone down to you! He is filled with fury, because he knows that his time is short"* (Revelation 12:12b). But thank God you are reading this now, so that you don't follow him there. Let Jesus save your soul, and if you are a backslider, come back to Father's house. Return to God and He will return to you.

Facts about Hell

Now let's look at some facts about heaven and hell from the Word of God. We'll look at hell first then go on to examine heaven.

1. Hell Is A Very Real Place

Whether you believe it or not does not change the fact. There is a real place called hell and it's terribly hot! You don't have to find out the hard way. Take precautions now. See to it that you don't go there.

Theologians tell us that Jesus taught more about hell than He did heaven. In Luke chapter 16, He narrates a true story about a rich man who died and went to hell. You can read it for yourself in full but here let us focus on verses 19 – 24.

"There was a rich man who was dressed in purple and fine linen and lived in luxury everyday. At his gate was laid a beggar named Lazarus, covered with sores and longing to eat what fell from the rich man's table. Even the dogs came and licked his sores. The time came when the beggar died and the angels carried him to Abraham's side. The rich man also died and was buried. In hell, where he was in torment, he looked up and saw Abraham far away, with Lazarus by his side. So he called to him, 'Father Abraham have pity on me and send Lazarus to dip the tip of his finger in water and cool my tongue, because I am in agony in this fire.'"

Now God has given us enough warnings about eternal punishment because He does not want us to follow the devil there. The fact that you are alive today is testimony that God has given you chance to repent and turn to Him. It is the mercy of God providing you an opportunity to make things right with Him. There are some people who believe that there is no hell or that hell is simply a myth. But friends, you can't take that risk. You cannot afford to stake your life on such an unfounded hope. Why should you discover the hard way when it's too late? Face the fact now and repent so that you can escape.

2. Hell Is A Place of Torment

"...send Lazarus to dip the tip of his finger in water and cool my tongue, because I am in agony in this fire" (Luke 16:24)

You can see in the Luke 16 passage that hell is not the grave and it's certainly not a fairy tale. That place is real and is burning hot right now. The rich man acknowledges the fact that he's in agony because of the intense fire of hell. One cannot express the deep regret that this man felt as he thought of the opportunity he missed to know God while he was still on earth. The remorse of his soul is practically indescribable. Now we all know that no one in their right mind would hold their hand over a candle flame for even five seconds. Now imagine a more intense heat all over your body and even on your tongue. You see how unbearable that sounds. It's horrible to imagine, but it's even worse in hell. Yet those in hell are awaiting a still greater punishment – the fiery lake of fire after the judgment. I know this is not a popular subject but we need to talk about it. Some of the most unpopular subjects in the bible are some of the most helpful.

3. Hell Is A Place without Mercy

"...Father Abraham, have pity on me..." (Luke 16:24).

There is no mercy for those in hell. It is impossible to show mercy to them, because they are now beyond redemption. They had their chance but they lost it. Perhaps many of them thought that they could repent later thinking there was still time or that they could repent quickly at the last minute. But without knowing what hit them, they found themselves sinking into the depths of hell. They wished they had even five seconds to confess Jesus as Lord but now it was too late. That is not what God wants for you, me or anyone else. He wants us to take heed to the warning now and commit our lives fully to the Lord.

4. Hell Was Created For the Devil and His Angels

Hell and the lake of fire were never created for human beings. They was created for the devil and his angels. *"Then He will say to those on His left, 'Depart from me, you who are cursed, into the eternal fire prepared for the devil and his angels"* (Matthew 25:14). The Devil knows his fate and he wants to take as many people with him as possible. He is competing for the same souls as we are. The bible says *"...He is filled with fury, because he knows that his time is short"* (Revelation 12:12b). Therefore let us not stand idle and watch Satan take people to hell. We must pray and labor to rescue as many souls as possible.

5. Hell Is Located Inside the Earth

Hell is located in what is known as the underworld. It is a massive place inside the earth where the bottomless pit and the lake of fire are found as well. The bible in Isaiah 14:9 and 15 says, *"Hell from beneath is moved for thee to meet thee at thy coming: It stirreth up the dead for thee...Yet thou shalt be brought down to hell, to the sides of the pit."* So hell is beneath and hell is down. Okay, enough about hell. Let's now talk about heaven.

Facts about Heaven

1. Heaven Is A Place of Indescribable Beauty

> *"I saw the Holy City, the new Jerusalem, coming down out of heaven from God, prepared as a bride beautifully dressed for her husband...It shone with the glory of God, and its brilliance was like that of a very precious jewel, like a jasper, clear as crystal"* (Revelation 21:2,11).

The most beautiful sunset cannot begin to compare with the indescribable beauty of heaven. The most awesome scene on earth comes no where near the least place in heaven. The art and architecture of heaven is simply beyond words. It has streets of pure transparent gold, pearly gates, walls of jasper, a crystal clear river of the water of life, and beautiful lush gardens that are breathtaking to say the least. Now who would want to miss that place? Who wouldn't want to be forever in God's presence enjoying the very best of what He created? This is our eternal hope my friends. It is our Father's inheritance for us.

2. Heaven Is a Place of Rapturous Praise and Worship

If you read the book of Revelation, you'll discover numerous instances where angels and people sing praises and worship God. There are beings up there who never cease to worship God saying, *"...Holy, holy, holy is the Lord God Almighty, who was, and is, and is to come"* (Revelation 4:8b). The 24 elders are seen casting their crowns at the Master's feet in praise and adoration for Him. This has got to be the greatest privilege in heaven as no other thing can compare to it. But we thank God that we don't have to wait till then. We can worship God now in spirit and truth. Let us rejoice and be glad and sing praises to the Lamb!

3. Heaven Is A Place of Unspeakable Joy

The greatest joy of heaven will be to see God face to face, for in His presence we will experience fullness of joy and at His right hand pleasures ever more. The Bible says God rejoices over you with singing and it will be wonderful to see God sing and for you (Zephaniah 3:17). You will laugh and laugh and laugh with God, for He who sits in heaven laughs (Psalm 2:4).

The second greatest joy of heaven will be the souls you influenced for the Lord and brought to Him. Heaven will be one great continuous party where everyone is happy and fulfilled forever. The souls you led to Jesus will be among those who will welcome you into everlasting habitations (Luke16:9). The Apostle Peter also admonishes us to do what it takes in order to *"...receive a rich welcome into the eternal kingdom of our Lord and Savior Jesus Christ"* (2 Peter 1:11). It will be better than any red carpet welcome you've ever seen. Don't miss any part of it.

4. Heaven Is a Place of Eternal Perfection

It is a place where not only the infrastructure is perfect, but the inhabitants also are perfected so that their relationships with one another are 100% peaceful and loving. It is a place where the environmental conditions are absolutely perfect. There are no problems whatsoever. There never will be a time when a crisis sets in. There is never going to be a boring moment.

There are no dead plants in heaven. The plants and animals there are full of life. The lions, tigers and other animals are all harmless and friendly. There is nothing that can harm or destroy. You don't sweat or get tired. It's a world where everything is working in perfect order.

5. Heaven Is a Place of Unending Fellowship

Now if there is anything to look forward to in heaven besides worshipping God, it is fellowshipping with His people. It will be wonderful to be reunited with the many people we knew while we were on earth. It will be the greatest family reunion ever.

How wonderful it will be to meet Abraham, Moses, David, Paul and many others who are among the great cloud of witnesses (Hebrews 12:1). You will want to ask Esther about how it was like in her time. You will want to see the many writers and people whose stories inspired you in the bible. We will have all the time to know each other better.

Heaven is a place of indescribable glory just like hell is a place of unimaginable horror.

How To Be Truly Sure You Will Enter Heaven

There are many Christians and even whole denominations that believe that you cannot know for sure whether or not you will be admitted into heaven when this life is over. They dwell on isolated verses of scripture which seem to suggest that only a few will make it while the vast majority will be cast into a hopeless eternity. This belief has unfortunately robbed many a Christian of the greatest hope they could have this side of eternity. It's sad because it makes God look like a lying politician who promises a better life at election time but abandons his supporters after being elected.

My dear friend, if there is anyone whose word you can truly rely on, it is God's. His are the surest, most certain and most reliable promises in the universe and forever more. What makes His promises so reliable is the fact that He is faithful and true. He has never and will never disappoint anyone. I like what the Bible says in respect of Sarah who trusted God to enable her to conceive and give birth to a baby boy despite her old age and barrenness. The bible tells us she had this faith *"because she considered [God] Who had given her the promise to be reliable and trustworthy and true to His word"* (Hebrews 11:11b AMP). I mean if there is anything impossible for the living God, it is for Him to lie or change His mind. If He ever did that, He would cease to be God. You see, Jesus doesn't just tell the truth, He is the Truth! He can't help but tell the truth as naturally as Satan tells lies because he is a liar and the father of lies. So when God says you are saved and guaranteed a place in heaven, do you suppose He is pleased when you and I doubt him? This is not a game of chance where you may or you may not. God cannot gamble with anything, especially not your life with regard to eternity. He is too serious about it to leave you unsure. God wants you and I to be 100% sure that not only are we saved with eternal life right now, but that we are citizens of heaven right now as though we were physically resident there. Our heavenly citizenship is in fact more real and more certain than our national one. A national citizen will among other evidences have a National Registration Card or Birth Certificate to prove his citizenship. But a heavenly citizen has at least three important proofs of his citizenship. These are described for us as follows:

1. Faith In The Finished Work of Christ

The very first reason I know I am a child of God who is guaranteed heaven is because I believe that Jesus Christ is the Son of God who died and rose again to reconcile me to God. *"Because if you acknowledge and confess with your lips that Jesus is Lord and in your heart believe (adhere to, trust in, and rely on the truth) that God raised Him from the dead, you will be saved"* (Romans 10:9 AMP). You can only become a citizen of heaven by accepting Jesus Christ as your Lord. This process of becoming a child of God is what Jesus called being 'born again.' In fact, it's interesting to note that He said this to a prominent religious leader of Israel. *"Jesus answered him, I assure, most solemnly I tell you, that unless a person is born again (anew, from above), he cannot ever see (know, be acquainted with, and experience) the kingdom of God."* John 3:3 AMP The phrase 'born again' is not a certain type of Christian or a church denomination. It is a spiritual experience resulting in our becoming children of God. We are in effect born of God. This born again experience is the only way to be a Christian. Being born in a Christian family and going to church does not make you a Christian. To be a Christian you must truly believe that Jesus gave His life for you and then confess Him as your Lord. When this occurs it means you are now born again. When you confess Jesus as Lord, the Holy Spirit recreates your human spirit in the image of God, after His likeness of righteousness, holiness and love. The life of God is now abiding in you. You have now become, a saint of God, a new creation in Christ, a child of God, and a citizen of heaven. The bible even says you have become the righteousness of God in Christ Jesus. You are saved!

So this confession of my faith in the finished work of Christ is my number one reason to rejoice that my name is recorded in the Book of Life and will remain there for as long as I do not forsake my faith. So my heavenly citizenship is no less real now as it will be on that day. I am a citizen of heaven not by my works but by faith in Christ Jesus my Lord. I know I am a Christian on my way to heaven because I have accepted the finished work of Christ on my behalf by faith.

2.   Love For The Brethren

The second reason I can have assurance that I have eternal life right now and a glorious future with Christ is because I love the brethren. The time I accepted Jesus as my Lord, His love nature was birthed in me and because of that I am able to love like He does. Listen to how the Amplified Bible puts it: *"We know that we have passed over out of death into Life by the fact that we love the brethren (our fellow Christians). He who does not love abides (remains, is held and kept continually) in [spiritual] death"* (1 John 3:14 AMP). Love is the greatest characteristic of God and is inevitably the most evident one (or at least should be) in the life of a child of God. God is love and since we are made in His image it naturally follows that we too possess His love nature. In fact Jesus said that our love for one another is our greatest witness to the world. What's more, love for one another is our new commandment given to us by our Lord Jesus (John 13:34-35) This love fulfills all the requirements of the law and is the supreme law of the universe. Thank God we can know we are saved and heaven-bound because of the evidence of His love shed abroad in our hearts by the Holy Spirit.

3. The Witness of the Holy Spirit within Me

The third reason I can be certain of my salvation and entry into heaven is by the witness of the Holy Spirit who lives inside my spirit. *"The Spirit Himself [thus] testifies together with our own spirit, [assuring us] that we are children of God"* (Romans 8:16 AMP). The Holy Spirit together with my recreated human spirit witness together that I am a child of God. Why would I question my salvation if the Holy Spirit continually assures me of it? Yet as though that was not enough, the bible also tells us that the Holy Spirit in us is a deposit guaranteeing our eternal inheritance. *"That [Spirit] is the guarantee of our inheritance [the firstfruits, the pledge and foretaste, the down payment on our heritage], in anticipation of its full redemption and our acquiring [complete] possession of it – to the praise of His glory"* (Ephesians 1:14 AMP). This should be overwhelming evidence with regard to your present salvation and an ever more blissful eternity with the Lover of your soul. The Holy Spirit is in you, to among other things, constantly remind you that you are a child of God. He is actually preparing you for eternity!

The Book of Life

> *"He who overcomes will, like them, be dressed in white. I will never blot out his name from the Book of Life, but will acknowledge his name before my Father and his angels"* (Revelation 3:5).

The Bible here speaks of a special record book where the name of every soul that belongs to Jesus is listed. This book contains the name of every holy person since the time of Adam. In fact while we are at this, let me ask you a very personal question. Do you have full assurance in your heart that your name is recorded in the Book of Life? Take a moment to think about it. If you don't have that assurance, then you need to get alone with God and pray. You will never know until you have made Jesus the Lord of your life and are walking with Him in close communion daily. The Holy Spirit will bear witness with your spirit that you indeed are a son of God. But if you haven't surrendered your life to Jesus, you will have no such assurance. Then again for those who at one time knew the Lord, but are not following Him anymore, I appeal to you in the name of the Lord Jesus to return to your Father's house. Like the prodigal son in Jesus' parable, it's time to leave the pig-pen and come back to Daddy. "Oh, but I can't do that because people have criticized and condemned me to where I don't think God Himself even bothers about me," somebody says. Well, let me tell you something my friend. The very fact that you are alive and reading this book right now means God loves you enough to give you an opportunity to repent and be restored. Besides, you are not the first backslider to return to Jesus. There've been many who've done worse things than you and even felt far worse than you might ever feel about yourself. Personally, I would hate to see you die in that condition and have to face God with the realization that you squandered this golden opportunity to be reconciled to Him. If I were you, I would pause right at this moment and pray to ask the Father to restore me to fellowship with Himself in Jesus' name. Don't waste any more time. Do so now! Say to Him, "Father, I'm sorry for turning my back on you. Forgive me I pray and restore me to the sweet fellowship I once knew. Help me to live for you until the day you call me home in Jesus' name." If you've sincerely done that, I have no doubt that you have full heart assurance that your name is recorded in that wonderful book. Welcome back! You can now *rejoice that your names are written in heaven"* (Luke 10:20).

Delivered From the Wrath to Come

When God was about to pour out His wrath on Sodom and Gomorrah, He first discussed the matter with His covenant friend Abraham. When Abraham realized what was about to happen to those wicked cities, he appealed to God's mercy with regard to the few righteous people who dwelt there. Abraham was convinced that God would not pour out His wrath on the righteous in the process of destroying the wicked. So in talking with God, Abraham said, *"Far be it from You to do such a thing –*

to slay the righteous with the wicked, so that the righteous fare as do the wicked! Far be it from You! Shall not the Judge of all the earth execute judgment and do righteously?" (Gen 18:25 AMP). When you read the full story, you'll discover that God rescued the righteous family of Lot before fire rained down on the wicked. You'll also find out that as the angels were taking Lot and his family out to safety, one of the angels remarked that judgment would not fall until Lot's family were away from the danger zone. I believe it's not hard to see how merciful and gracious God is.

The reason I brought up this story is so that we can see how, even now, God has warned us through His word about the wrath to come during the great tribulation and worse still at the Great White Throne Judgment. God in no way wants you or me to experience it anymore than He wanted Lot and his family to be destroyed with the wicked. The God who always makes a way of escape has given us the greatest and only Way in the Person of Jesus. I want the following statement to be indelibly printed in your memory: we have been delivered from the wrath to come through the blood of Jesus! I want you to meditate on it and loudly declare this statement over and over until you are fully convinced of its truth.

The fact of our deliverance from the wrath to come is very firmly stated for us in 1 Thessalonians 1:10 (AMP): *"And [how you] look forward to and await the coming of His Son from heaven, whom He raised from the dead – Jesus, Who personally rescues and delivers us out of and from the wrath [bringing punishment] which is coming [upon the impenitent] and draws us to Himself [investing us with all the privileges and rewards of the new life in Christ, the Messiah]."* Thank God we are delivered from the wrath to come! God is not trying to punish you and He's not looking forward to it. He's not some mean old headmaster with a stick in hand waiting for you to make the slightest mistake so he can cane you. *"For God has not appointed us to [incur His] wrath [He did not select us to condemn us] but [that we might] obtain [His] salvation through our Lord Jesus Christ [the Messiah]"* (1 Thessalonians 5:9 AMP).

My friend if you are still not sure that God has delivered us from the wrath to come, here's a verse of scripture that should settle this issue beyond the shadow of a doubt: *"Therefore, since we are now justified (acquitted, made righteous, and brought into right relationship with God) by Christ's blood, how much more [certain is it that] we shall be saved by Him from the indignation and wrath of God"* (Roman 5:9 AMP). So there you have it! Now that you are a new creature in Christ Jesus, you can rest assured that your deliverance from the wrath to come is absolutely guaranteed. I rest my case!

What If I Fall Away?

"Oh, but I am afraid I might fall away and be lost!" someone says. My friend, you have every right to be afraid if you are depending on your own strength. The Bible tells us that the One who saved us is also able to keep us from falling. Jude 24 (AMP) assures us, *"Now to Him Who is able to keep you without stumbling or slipping or falling, and to present [you] unblemished (blameless and faultless) before the presence of His glory in triumphant joy and exultation [with unspeakable, ecstatic delight)."* These are the sort of scriptures you should be dwelling on to establish your heart in the fact that your loving Father holds you up in His everlasting arms and no one can snatch you out of His eternally secure hands. He upholds you, and yes, even when you do stumble momentarily, He picks you up. He just can't give up on you even if you have given up on yourself. So you see that fear of falling is proof of a lack of faith in the One who not only saves but upholds all who believe. The God who saved you will also see to it that you get to heaven. Actually I don't think I can say it any better than the Apostle Paul did when he said, *"[And indeed] the Lord will certainly deliver and draw me to Himself from every assault of evil. He will preserve and bring me safe unto His heavenly kingdom. To Him be the glory forever and ever. Amen [so be it]"* (2 Timothy 4:18 AMP). So it's not a matter of hoping that somehow, by chance, you might eventually make it into heaven hanging on to a thread. No, my friend, you can have solid hope that our faithful Father guarantees your safe passage through this life and all the way to heaven. You should be dancing by now!

Are Only A Few People Going To Make It To Heaven?

Many have wondered whether only a few will make it to heaven while the greater masses will be lost. This question has for a long time bothered me as well. I have thought of the one particular Asian country whose population is over 1.2 billion people and just how many of them will make it to heaven. But as time went on I began to see that God is not a wasteful investor. He did not invest his Son in the earth only to reap a meager harvest. No, my friend, God is abundant and excellent at everything He does. If, like most theologians agree, God lost only a third of the angels at Satan's rebellion, what makes you think Satan will carry more souls with him to the lake of fire than God will to heaven? God forbid that that should happen!

But I wouldn't just want to speculate about it either. God has already told us how this whole matter concludes, and it's this: **when it's all said and done, we win!** By that I mean the vast majority will be in heaven as the following verses of scripture show us:

1. **Revelation 7:9:** *"After this I beheld, and lo, a great multitude, which no man could number, of all nations, and kindreds, and people, and tongues, stood before the throne, and before the Lamb, clothed with white robes, and palms in their hands."* John in his heavenly vision sees an ocean of humanity before God's throne who've all made it to heaven. This verse alone should be more than enough to assure us that heaven will be immensely populated to the glory of God.
2. **Hebrews 2:10:** *"For it became him, for whom are all things, and by whom are all things, in bringing many sons unto glory..."* God fully expected that by giving up His only begotten Son He would gain many sons as a result. I hope you notice it doesn't say few sons, but many. If you have accepted Jesus as your Lord, you are one of those many sons that have been brought to glory.

3. **Genesis 13:16:** *"And I will make thy seed as the dust of the earth: so that if a man can number the dust of the earth, then shall thy seed also be numbered."* God told Abraham that his natural and spiritual descendants would be incredibly numerous. At one time God even compared Abraham's descendants to the number of the stars in the heavens. In fact scientists today cannot tell the number of the stars. You, according to Galatians 3:7 are one of Abraham's innumerable descendants. Heaven's population will be as countless as the dust of the earth!

4. **Isaiah 53:11:** *"He shall see of the travail of his soul, and shall be satisfied: by his knowledge shall my righteous servant justify many; for he shall bear their iniquities."* This is a prophecy about the result that would follow the sacrificial death of Jesus and His subsequent resurrection. The result would be the salvation of so many people that Jesus Himself would be satisfied that His sacrifice was worth it in every way.

Now, let's look at it this way: apart from the many people who will turn to Christ, there are already myriads that are in heaven right now beginning with Adam's generation. The number of babies and little children under the age of accountability who have died since then should number in the billions. Miscarried and aborted babies all have been received into heaven because Jesus Himself said that of such is the kingdom of heaven (Mark 10:13-16). I am more than convinced that all the (human) babies and children who died in Noah's flood, Sodom and Gomorrah, the world wars and as a result of any other reason since Adam all made it to heaven in their billions. Then we have the untold billions of adults who believed in the one true God from Eden to the cross who are now a part of the great cloud of witnesses in heaven. Add to those, the multitudes who've gotten saved since the thief on the cross to-date. Then finally there will be billions more born during the 1000 year reign of Christ on earth who will enter the eternal perfect state with us. I'm sure you are beginning to see why heaven will be immensely populated. You just have to be there!

End-Times: A Message of Hope

It is sad that the greatest hope of the saints has at times been undermined by unbalanced teachings coming from well-meaning preachers who do not realize the great damage they are doing to the body of Christ. Hope, together with faith and love are the three greatest virtues that we are to aspire for. But if you listen to a lot of end-time teaching you'll be more scared of facing the future than you were if you hadn't listened. This is just not right.

The gospel, which is good news, includes God's great and glorious plans for your future. He, like He says in Jeremiah 29:11, has plans to prosper us and not to harm us. He goes on to say that He has plans to give us hope and an expected end or desirable future. Over and over God keeps telling us in His word that He wants us to experience His abundant blessings both in this life and the next. So doom and gloom preaching about the end times is just not balanced. We need to emphasize the victory of Christ above all the negative events of the last days. In fact, by the time Jesus comes for us, we will be in far greater shape than when we started. We will be the glorious church He's always envisioned.

Don't spend much of your time dwelling on the negative signs of the last days which are all over the news. Rather pay particular attention to what God is doing to advance His kingdom on earth. You will begin to see the multitudes of people who are turning away from Satan to God. You will see the many Christians who are taking their rightful place and representing Jesus in every field of endeavor – education, media, politics, business and law among many others. You will rejoice as you see God's people becoming more prosperous than we've ever been. Truly, even as the world is experiencing greater darkness than ever, the Church is shining the brightest. The glory of God is being seen on us now more than ever! (Isaiah 60:1-3)

CHAPTER 5

THE MINISTRY OF EVERY BELIEVER

"For we are God's workmanship, created in Christ Jesus to do good works, which God prepared in advance for us to do" (Ephesians 2:10).

We are not saved by works, but we are saved to do good works. Our works of service will be evaluated by the Lord to determine what our reward will be. It is therefore important that we know what these good works are in order to make the most of our lives. Our good works must actually be an outward expression of the life of God in us. *"For it is God who works in you to will and to act according to His good purpose"* (Philippians 2:13).

The motive behind the action is as important as the action itself. The works of service that will not burn up on that day are the ones done out of love for the Master and for the people He created for Himself. It is works that are done for His glory and not for the praises of men. The works that will burn are the ones done from selfish motives to impress men. That is why one deed of service done out of love outweighs one million acts done for the approval of men. Surely we must do a lot for the kingdom, but let's make sure it's all done out of love. It's not the quantity but the quality that comes first. For *"If I give all I possess to the poor and surrender my body to the flames, but have not love, I gain nothing"* (1 Corinthians 13:3). The value of every action is tied to the motive behind it. So make sure that *"whatever you do, whether in word or deed, do it in the name of the Lord Jesus, giving thanks to God the Father through Him"* (Colossians 3:17).

Our willingness to serve is also an important factor in determining the quality of our work. We must serve wholeheartedly and joyfully, not halfheartedly and with a sour attitude. God wants us to be willing to do His will and not feel obligated to do it out of a mere sense of duty. He wants us to evangelize, pray, serve in church and help other people because we want to and not because we feel forced. If we do something good without a willing heart I doubt if it will pass the fire test at the judgment. It doesn't bless a parent to have their child unwillingly obey them, does it? Or if your husband or wife told you they did something for you simply to get you off their back, would that please you? So in the same way it won't please God for us to do our work unwillingly. Our heart must be in what we do or else it's not worth doing.

Our waiting for the Lord must not be passive but active. Almost every verse that speaks about Christ's return, emphasizes that we are to do something until He comes. We are to be praying, winning the lost, helping the poor, or serving in one way or another. We are not to just sit idly by and wait for Him to come. No, we are to do kingdom business until He comes (Luke 19:13 KJV). We must maximize every opportunity that comes our way and use our gifts for His glory even as we see the day approaching. *"Therefore, as we have opportunity, let us do good to all people, especially to those who belong to the family of believers"* (Galatians 6:10).

The 24 Works of Righteousness

"Fine linen, bright and clean, was given her to wear. [Fine linen stands for the righteous acts of the saints.]" (Revelation 19:8).

"Be careful not to do your 'acts of righteousness' before men, to be seen by them. If you do, you will have no reward from your Father in heaven" (Matthew 6:1).

There are many good works we are called to do but I have selected twenty-four of them to help us get started in our service for the Master. I encourage you to study them, and do them so that you can make a difference in this world for the kingdom of God. These are the works that will follow you to the judgment seat, so do them with all your heart. You can also look at them as 24 Ways to Invest in Eternity for this is indeed what they are. The returns on these investments are eternal.

1. Soul Winning

> *"Those who are wise will shine like the brightness of the heavens, and those who lead many to righteousness, like the stars forever and ever"* (Daniel 12:3).

The greatest responsibility ever given to man is to rescue people from eternal destruction. The soul of man is more precious beyond anything in all creation. The value of a soul is incalculable because the price paid for it was the infinitely valuable blood of Jesus. This makes a soul most precious above any created thing.

The reward of a soul winner is one of the greatest in heaven. The souls we bring to Him will qualify us for the beautiful soul winner's crown. We will shine brightly like the stars forever and ever. This is the reward of the soul winner. So let us strive to bring as many lost souls to Jesus as possible. Let us ask for wisdom and boldness to go out and preach the gospel through every available means. If you are very timid, go and work with someone who's already successful at winning souls. Do not be ashamed of the gospel, but step out in faith. You have a soul winner's crown to win.

2. Praying For Others

> *"I urge, then, first of all, that requests, prayers, intercession and thanksgiving be made for everyone – for kings and all those in authority, that we may live peaceful and quiet lives in all godliness and holiness. This is good, and pleases God our Savior, who wants all men to be saved and to come to a knowledge of the truth"* (1 Timothy 2:1-3).

Prayer is so important to the work of the ministry that without it, we can forget about fulfilling the will of God. The vitality of prayer cannot be overemphasized. It is as vital as oxygen is to our lungs.

The Bible admonishes us over and over to pray consistently for God's will to be done. It tells us to pray for our national leaders so that we can have a peaceful atmosphere for preaching the gospel. He wants us through prayer to release His purposes and establish them on earth. Our prayers for ourselves and others will do more for the kingdom of God than almost any one thing. They will release laborers into the harvest to reap souls for the Kingdom. I personally believe some of the greatest rewards in heaven will go to those who prayed faithfully for God's purposes to be accomplished. Will you be one of them?

3. Giving To the Poor

> *"...Your prayers and gifts to the poor have come up as a memorial offering before God"* (Acts 10:4b).

Giving to the poor is lending to the Lord and the Lord will pay us back with blessings in this life and rewards in eternity. Many of us have clothes we hardly ever wear, shoes we almost never put on and extra supplies of food that we can pass on to those less privileged. Giving to the poor must not be done as an afterthought. It must be planned. Think of how many poor people you could help if you included them on your monthly spending plan. Just imagine yourself setting aside some money for a poor person's groceries each month. Such an investment will make life worth living. Let us not ignore the poor among us but let us reach out to them with our resources and God's love. Our attitude towards the poor is our attitude towards God. We must be generous and share with those in need and we shall have treasure in heaven.

4. Remembering Those in Prison

"Remember those in prison as if you were their fellow prisoners, and those who are mistreated as if you yourselves were suffering" (Hebrews 13:3).

It is important that the gospel reaches the dark corners of every nation including prisons. We must step out to provide food and other supplies to those in prison together with the message of salvation through Jesus Christ. Those people do not have an opportunity to go to church like we do, so church has to be taken to them. We must get a lot of good Christian literature together with bibles and supply them to every prison we can. We can initiate programs of prison outreach or support already established programs doing the same.

5. Caring For Widows

"Religion that God our Father accepts as pure and faultless is this: to look after orphans and widows in their distress..." (James 1:27).

Christianity must get out of the four walls of the church building and get its hands dirty helping those in need. We must as individual believers and churches begin to address the plight of the widows among us. Surely many of us can include them on our monthly budget so that they can pay rentals and buy groceries. Perhaps you can commit to buying a widow a pack of groceries every month and as the Lord increases your income, you can include more widows on your list. That's the way to do church outside of the church building. Some of us can even sponsor these widows to learn a trade or assist them start a business or even give them a job. All these acts of kindness will further the kingdom and go towards your reward in heaven. In fact I think it's a good idea to send some of these widows to bible school. The things you can do for them are practically endless.

6. Taking Care of Orphans

"Religion that God our Father accepts as pure and faultless is this: to look after orphans and widows in their distress..." (James 1:27).

God has called us not only to preach but also to meet the needs of the vulnerable. The Lord has given us the mandate to look after the orphans among us. He wants us to provide them with godly parental care the way we do our own children. I am reminded of George Muller the famous preacher of the 1800s who built five large orphanages in England that took care of thousands of orphans. I believe some us could do the same, while others of us can sponsor an orphan's education or even adopt one into our family. Use your money and other resources to do something worthwhile for the kingdom while you can. I believe we, the Christians ought to be at the forefront of helping the disadvantaged in society. Think seriously of what you can do to better the lives of others. They may not pay you back, but the Lord will repay you handsomely at the resurrection of the just. But don't forget, He will also bless you mightily in this life. Taking care of orphans is one of the greatest ways to demonstrate the love of the Father to the world. We will convince more people to turn to Christ if we demonstrate the gospel through acts of kindness.

7. Helping the Homeless

"...I was a stranger and you invited me in" (Mathew 25:35b).

The people living on the street are not just the government's responsibility. They are the church's responsibility as well. Yes, even the refugees driven from their home countries need our help. The body of Christ should take a leading role in dealing with such kinds of humanitarian crises. We must arise and take our place of responsibility in addressing social needs. Homeless children and adults out there need our help. You or I could be God's answer to someone else's prayer. We are God's solution to society's ills. The homeless are crying for a home. Who will raise revenue to build them a home? Who will surrender a piece of property to accommodate them and minister to their other needs? Who will tell them Jesus loves them by providing a roof over their heads? Tell me who, if not you and I? Just imagine what sort of impact Christianity would have if we put our resources together and provided shelter for the homeless of our society. The world would not ignore us. They would want to know this love.

8. Assisting the Disabled

> *"But when you give a banquet, invite the poor, the crippled, the lame, the blind, and you will be blessed. Although they cannot repay you, you will be repaid at the resurrection of the righteous"* (Luke 14: 13-14).

That scripture is a call to social action for the church. If we faithfully reached out to these people both spiritually and materially it wouldn't be long before we got the world's attention. They would want to know why we are so compassionate and we can tell them about Jesus. By our actions we can help them experience God's love. God has promised to reward us for every kind act towards the disabled among us. He will bless us in this life and reward us on that day.

9. Helping the Aged

You don't have to look around very long to find a ministry opportunity. They are everywhere. Somebody near you needs your help. You may not realize it, but God has appointed you and I to be His agents of compassion in the earth. We are called to love like He loves. He wants us to reach out to the neglected elderly people of this world. He wants us to lead them to Christ and help them do His will in the little time they have left. He wants us to prepare them for a great home-going to heaven. We must reach out to these grey-haired people and not only minister to them spiritually but also take care of their material needs. Let us treat them the way we would our beloved parents in their old age. I think I don't have to tell you that there's a reward for that.

10. Providing for the Hungry and Thirsty

"For I was hungry and you gave me something to eat, I was thirsty and you gave me something to drink..." (Matthew 25:35).

One of the greatest definitions of love I've ever heard is simply this: sharing and caring. There are a lot of people who hardly have anything to eat or drink. They need someone to reach out to them with not only the salvation message but with food supplies and something to drink. This is the kind of Christianity the world has been waiting for. The bible tells us that God will even reward such simple acts like giving a cup of cold water to one of His disciples. We need to redefine the way we do ministry if we are to fulfill the great commission.

11. Clothing the Naked

"I needed clothes and you clothed me..." (Matthew 25:36).

When Jesus delivered the naked and mad man of the Gerasenes, He did not just leave him naked as He found him. No. The Bible says that when the people in the region came to see what had happened *"...they found the man from whom the demons had gone out, sitting at Jesus' feet, dressed and in His right mind..."* (Luke 8:35). Many of us have wardrobes jam-packed with clothes and shoes some of which we hardly ever wear. We need to go through our wardrobe and select items we can give to those who desperately need clothing. Let us cover the nakedness of everyone we can as we reach out to them with the gospel of Christ. The Bible says, *"If anyone has material possessions and sees his brother in need but has no pity on him, how can the love of God be in him? Dear children, let us not love with words or tongue but with actions and in truth"* (1 John 3:17-18) Let us share with others in love. Let us not be selfish or stingy. That is not God's nature. Let the world see God's love demonstrated through you. Of course your motive mustn't be to impress men but to glorify your Father in heaven. People are usually very open to what you have to say once they know you care.

12. Looking After the Sick

"...I was sick and you looked after me..." (Matthew 25:36).

The sick need our help and it is our responsibility to minister to them. We should take care of them and take God's healing power to them. A lot of sick people will be healed and receive Jesus as their Lord but many will only need someone to lead them to Jesus right on their death bed. Let us do all we can to minister to the sick among us. These include not just our friends and relatives but the many people lying sick in hospital beds and at home. We shouldn't wait for them to call for our help. We can take the initiative to minister God's love and healing to them. Some of them don't have adequate beddings, or food and many can hardly pay their medical bills. This is where you and I come in as God's ministers of mercy.

13. Exercising Hospitality

"Do not forget to entertain strangers, for by so doing some people have entertained angels without knowing it" (Hebrews 13:2).

Many of us meet people we don't know on a regular basis and the Bible tells us how to treat these strangers. We must open our hearts to be a blessing to people we do not know. But that does not mean we should let anybody take advantage of our kindness. We must be wise as serpents but innocent as doves. That simply means we must follow our hearts and use our heads. That way we can use our kindness intelligently. Entertaining strangers the way we entertain our guests could very well open a door of spiritual ministry to them.

14. Doing Good to Your Enemies

"But I say unto you, Love your enemies, bless them that hate you, and pray for them which despitefully use you, and persecute you" (Matthew 5:44 KJV).

Jesus is here telling us to do something that we cannot do in our natural selves. He tells us to demonstrate mercy, love and kindness to those who are a thorn in our flesh. It is not that He wants to make our lives miserable, but that He wants us to put God's love to work so that we can minister to such people and reap heavenly rewards in the process. We don't have to do it through our own human effort but by the love that God has already shed abroad in our hearts by the Holy Spirit. It is His grace that will enable us to treat these people the way Jesus did. If we focus on His love, we will love our enemies like God does His. It takes natural love to love those who already love us, but supernatural love to love those who are hostile towards us. This love is not far away. It is within you if you have accepted Jesus as your Lord. You have more than enough love in you to love the most hateful person in the world and that's not your mother-in-law, even though you should love her dearly as well. You will be rewarded for demonstrating God's love to those who are difficult to love.

15. Restoring the Backslidden

"I will heal your backslidings" (Jeremiah 3:22).

It is very unfortunate that sometimes people who once accepted Jesus as their Lord and lived for Him no longer do so. They used to walk in the light but now they have turned their backs on Christ and are walking in darkness. These are commonly referred to as "backsliders," and the Lord has given each of us the responsibility of restoring them to fellowship with Himself and the Church.

First things first; we need to pray for their restoration asking the Lord to open their eyes again to see Him for who He is – a loving and compassionate Father who is waiting to embrace them. We can stand on the covenant promise that God will heal their backslidings. We can trust God that like the prodigal son, they will come to their senses and return to Father's house.

Then apart from praying for them, we should be available and willing to let God use us to reach them with His living-kindness and compassion. What such people need the most is unconditional acceptance and not rejection. We must also be patient, however, as for some it may take a while before they can make the decision to come back home. But as God's unfailing love is patient and kind, we should treat them as though they were already restored even as we await their actual restoration. Ours is to act in love towards them so that if they refuse to repent, we will have done our part and will be rewarded by God for our perseverance.

16. Tithing

> "Bring the whole tithe into the storehouse, that there may be food in my house. Test me in this, says the Lord Almighty, and see if I will not throw open the floodgates of heaven and pour out so much blessing that you will not have room enough for it" (Malachi 3:10).

The tithe, which is ten percent of your income, is one of the greatest opportunities you have for exercising financial stewardship before God. It is the primary way He gauges whether you can be entrusted with greater responsibility. If you are unfaithful in handling earthly riches, you can't be entrusted with the true spiritual riches Jesus talked about. The bible tells us that Jesus receives our tithes in heaven and so if we don't give our tithes, we are among other things denying ourselves the opportunity to store up riches in heaven. We are actually depriving ourselves of heavenly rewards. The faithful tither will experience benefits in this life and will also be richly rewarded in the next life. Every tithe you pay in this life will go to make up your eternal riches in heaven plus enable you to walk in the fullness of God's blessing in this very life. There apparently is a record of your tithes that's kept in heaven. How do you want it to look like when you finally get there?

17. Giving Offerings

The Word of God has much to say about our attitude towards material things and in particular money itself. Jesus told us that it is more blessed to give than to receive (Acts 20:35). It is not just the amount or act of giving that counts but the heart attitude of the giver. *"Every man according as he purposeth in his heart, so let him give; not grudgingly, or of necessity: for God loves a cheerful giver"* (2 Corinthians 9:7 KJV). God is telling us that giving is a heart issue. It is only when we give joyfully, motivated by God's love, that our giving honors God who will certainly reward it.

Do you remember the time when Jesus sat opposite the treasury and observed how the people cast money into the treasury? Many rich people put in huge amounts from the abundance that they had. But there was a poor widow who came and threw in two little copper coins which was all she had. Upon seeing this, Jesus spoke highly of the manner in which she gave – sacrificially (Matthew 12:41-44).

Now this does not mean that we should be giving away all our earnings but that our offering should be valuable enough to be considered a sacrifice. Hers was in the Lord's estimation the greatest offering not because of the amount but because of the heart behind it. A $1 offering given wholeheartedly in love as unto the Lord is greater than $1 million given grudgingly or for show to men. Big or small amount, the point is give with the right attitude or motive to glorify God and God alone. Our heart should truly be in our giving. This is the kind of giving our Lord loves to see. God is a heart God, and He wants our giving to come from the heart as a true act of worship, and not as an after-thought or a duty we feel obligated to perform.

Now there are many opportunities and causes to which we can give. These include weekly church offerings, church building funds, missions and so on. But it's missions-giving that I am more interested in elaborating on.

To me this is the wisest financial investment you can ever make in your life. People donate mega millions and billions of dollars towards many causes such as AIDS and cancer research, animal rights, space technology and political ideals to name a few. I am not against these causes but I feel sad that we as Christians have been donating far less to the greatest cause of all – soul-winning.

Jesus said in respect of this eternal investment, *"And I tell you, make friends for yourselves by means of unrighteous mammon [deceitful riches, money, possessions], so that when it fails, they [those you have favored] may receive you into everlasting habitations [dwellings]"* (Luke 16:9 AMP). This is an investment whose returns will never be lost but shall abide with you forever. You are in a sense converting money into souls for God's heavenly kingdom. I mean, what kind of investment could beat that? It is my appeal to every reader of this book to set aside some money every month, or however often you get money, and give it to evangelistic causes in your church or other soul winning outreaches outside of your own church. Surely if we gave more to missions and evangelized more ourselves, there would be such a mighty harvest of souls everywhere. We can do it and by God's grace we shall! Pastors, I urge you to set some money aside in your church budget for missions. In fact, it should be a top priority in every church or ministry budget.

18. Doing Your Job As Unto the Lord

In Ephesians 6:5-9 servants or employees are admonished to do their regular jobs as unto the Lord. They are told to serve wholeheartedly as though they were working directly for Christ. Then we are told how our daily jobs affect eternity: *"because you know that the Lord will reward everyone for whatever good he does, whether he is slave or free"* (Ephesians 6:8). So your job is not just a matter of getting paid at the month-end. It is a stewardship test to qualify you for eternal responsibility in the life to come. Your work performance is being assessed not just by your boss but by recording angels who record your daily activities on earth.

19. Volunteering To Serve In Your Local Church

In Ephesians chapter 4 the bible tells us that among other things the reason Jesus gave us apostles, prophets, evangelists, pastors and teachers was to develop the saints to do service in God's kingdom. Verse 12 in the Amplified bible makes this very clear. It says, *"His intention was the perfecting and the full equipping of the saints (His consecrated people), [that they should do] the work of ministering toward building up Christ's body (the church)."* Every one of us has

a role to play in the body of Christ at large and in our local church in particular.

Our churches are in need of faithful volunteers to serve in various areas such as

music, sound, cleaning, hospitality, greeting, ushering, counseling, visitation, cell groups, children, youth, trafflc, maintenance - the list is virtually endless. There is something that God has or is equipping you to do in your local church. There is a place where you can bloom and blossom to the benefit of that church and God's glory. If you are not sure where to start, ask the Lord to lead you and take steps to volunteer in the first department that comes to mind. Then as you begin serving, follow the leading in your heart until you have full assurance of where you can serve long-term.

It will be easier for you to find your place of service if you take a step to start. Do you remember Stephen and Phillip who started out serving in a position that required them to distribute food to widows? (Acts 6:1-7). Then as they faithfully served in this capacity, the Lord promoted them. Stephen went on to be a dynamic preacher working amazing miracles and became the first post-resurrection martyr recorded in scripture. Phillip became an evangelist traveling from place to place winning souls to Christ with miracles accompanying his preaching.

Both Stephen and Phillip started out serving in the local church and God promoted them to serve outside of the local church in due season. Their ministry outreach was simply an extension of the local church to the communities around. They were not simply using the food distribution ministry as a platform to launch out "their" ministry. No! They just served where they were until God promoted them. So let's keep our motives pure and truly serve as unto the Lord. It doesn't have to be something in the limelight that everyone can acknowledge and notice. You just do whatever it is – noticeable or not – as unto the Lord who rewards and promotes his faithful ones.

Your service under the local church and even your regular job during the week can be a great ministry unto the Lord if you do them as such.

> "And whatsoever ye do, do it heartily, as to the Lord and not unto men. Knowing that of the Lord ye shall receive the reward of the inheritance: for ye serve the Lord Christ" (Colossians 3:23-24 KJV).

20. Providing For Your Immediate Family

The family has a special place in God's plan as an oasis of love reflecting the love that the Father has for the Son. The human family is patterned after the divine family. Therefore as spouses and parents, we are called to demonstrate the Father's love to our spouses and children respectively. Every time we do that, we are allowing them and those that watch us to more clearly see what our Father God is really like. Generosity, like every other godly virtue, should be learned and practiced in the home as a matter of priority. I truly believe that our exemplary family life will attract more people to Jesus than we may ever know in this life. They are watching how we treat and care for each other. Remember, love is our greatest witness to the world that we are Christ's disciples.

God's best is that we all grow up in loving families that will shape our understanding of who God is – a loving and caring Provider. The father in the home is to take the lead in demonstrating God's love to His wife and kids through, among other things, providing for their basic needs. This apparently is so important that some of the strongest language in the bible is used against those who neglect their families. *"If anyone fails to provide for his relatives, especially for those of his own family, he has disowned the faith [by failing to accompany it with fruits] and is worse than an unbeliever [who performs his obligation in these matters]"* (1 Timothy 5:8 AMP) This is not to make those who may be struggling economically feel guilty about their current situation. Temporal setbacks are not to be taken into account. The bible is talking about those who just abandon their families or abrogate their God-given responsibility to support them. But thank God, that even during trying economic times, we have a heavenly Father whom we can rely on to bring us through. That is why as bread-winners we must always rely on our true Source of abundant supply.

21. Providing For Your Relatives

Uncles, aunts, cousins, nephews, nieces, and yes even our in-laws, are among the many relatives we must help take care of and reach out to with the gospel. Indeed to many of them our greatest witness will be our care and good treatment of them.

> *"If anyone fails to provide for his relatives, especially for those of his own family, he has disowned the faith [by failing to accompany it with fruits] and is worse than an*

unbeliever [who performs his obligation in these matters]"
(1 Timothy 5:8 AMP).

It is a shame to see non-believers act more responsibly towards their relatives than believers. Brethren, this ought not to be so. We who understand the heart of the Father and know His love should be the ones to lead by example. The world should see the character of our Father shining through us. Taking care of our relatives, like every other thing we do out of love to the glory of God is an investment for eternity. It may seem ordinary but it has extraordinary impact for the kingdom.

"Oh, but some of my relatives don't like me, especially my in-laws." Then do what Jesus said to do. Love them, do good to them, bless them and pray for them. Whether they respond to your love or not, love them anyway. Follow the golden rule. The bible says love never fails but endures all things without weakening (1 Corinthians 13:8). Most, if not all of them, will eventually be unable to resist that love and will have to respond. But even if they don't, you just love them all the way to the end. If they have a need, do whatever you can to meet it. Do not be overcome by evil but overcome evil with good (Romans 12:21). God will greatly reward you for treating them better than they deserved.

22. Supporting Your Pastor

Every one of us should belong to a local church where we meet regularly for fellowship with other believers and feed on God's word. The local church is our spiritual family led by a parental figure known scripturally as our pastor. The pastor's main job is to establish us in God's word so that we can mature into Christlikeness. Yet the pastor cannot fulfill his calling without our help. He needs our moral, spiritual and material support for him to succeed in his calling.

"Let him who received instruction in the Word [of God] share all good things with his teacher [contributing to his support]"

(Galatians 6:6 AMP). It is essential that our pastor is well catered for financially so that he can do his job single-mindedly. Let us not forget that his first obligation is to his family and then the church. So we as the local church should see to it that he is well housed, has proper transportation, more than enough food and clothes for the family and adequate funds to even afford a vacation. We must never let him be under financial pressure because that will not work to our advantage anyway. In fact, apart from giving our pastor a salary, we as individual church members should take it upon ourselves to give something extra to supplement his income. We should do this because we truly love him as God wants us to. I guess I don't have to tell you that you will share in his heavenly reward.

Another very important way to support our pastor is to pray for him regularly. Our mouth should never be used to gossip about him but to uphold him and his family in prayer. Our prayer support is the greatest support we can render towards the fulfillment of his call. Even the Apostle Paul on more than one occasion solicited the prayer support of believers, many of whom he had led to Christ himself. In 1 Thessalonians 5:25 he asked the believers, *"Brethren, pray for us."* Then in Ephesians 6:19-20 of the Amplified Bible he says, *"And (pray) also for me, that (freedom of) utterance may be given me, that I may open my mouth to proclaim boldly the mystery of the good news (the Gospel), For which I am an ambassador in a coupling chain (in prison. Pray) that I may declare it boldly and courageously as I ought to do."* So let us not grow weary in praying for our pastors, for it is through prayer support that the work of the Lord will be accomplished. Then on that day in heaven, you will see just how much your prayers have accomplished.

23. Honoring Your Parents

"Honor [esteem and value as precious] your father and mother –this is the first commandment with a promise – That all may be well with you and that you may live long on the earth" (Ephesians 6:2-3 AMP).

I know some of us may not know our biological parents or may have lost them a while back but there are people in our lives right now who act in a parental role towards us such as our mentors.

The bible tells us that by honoring our parents, guardians, or parental figures we will experience a long life where things go well for us. This honor can be accorded in many different ways such us speaking respectfully to and about them, giving them financial support, spending quality time learning from them and simply enjoying their company, praying for them, and giving them gifts. Jesus once rebuked some religious leaders for devising a clever way of neglecting this responsibility (Mark 7:9-13). If Jesus rebuked men for neglecting to honor their parents, He definitely will commend and reward those who honor them. That means you could lose rewards for neglecting this responsibility.

The Bible, speaking in respect of widows (who are parents) says, "But if a widow has children or grandchildren, these should learn first of all to put their religion into practice by caring for their own family and so repaying their parents and grandparents, for this is pleasing to God." (1 Timothy 5:4). Now what's pleasing to God? It is the fact that the children or grandchildren demonstrate God's love by taking good care of their parents and grannies. Even though the context speaks in respect of taking care of widows, the underlying message is still the same – honor.

24. Mourning with Those Who Mourn

"Rejoice with those who rejoice; mourn with those who mourn" (Romans 12:15).

In this life we will face situations that will cause us to mourn such as funerals and broken relationships among others. Many times the best thing to do for a person who is mourning is not to try and give them advice but "a shoulder to lean and cry on." That means giving them a listening and sympathetic ear so that they can have an emotional release.

Mourning with those who mourn is a much needed ministry of comfort in this world of trials and tribulations. Someone who has just lost a spouse, a child, a job, or has suffered humiliation via a scandal needs the reassuring presence of a comforting friend who truly cares. This may not be the time to say, "Here's a bible verse," but to simply be the goodness and loving-kindness of God surrounding that person. A person who has just undergone a devastating divorce needs moral and spiritual support – not condemnation. What they need is to know that someone cares. This is how people can bounce back from life's temporal setbacks.

To mourn with those who mourn is to act like our Lord Jesus who according to Hebrews 4:15 is touched with the feelings of our infirmities. I believe one way the Lord comforts us is through the loving presence of our brothers and sisters in Christ. This doesn't mean you have a pity party but that the support we provide for the one mourning helps them up again. Two will always be better than one. That's how God designed life.

CHAPTER 6

JUDGE YOURSELF

"So in everything, do to others what you would have them do to you, for this sums up the Law and the Prophets" (Matthew 7:12).

The golden rule is the golden key to achieving greatness in the kingdom of God. It is the number one rule to follow in all the relationships we have. It is referred to by James as the royal law (of love) or the law of the kingdom (James 2:8). If our number one priority is not love - both for God and for man – then whatever we accomplish in life is all in vain. We will most certainly disqualify ourselves from God's high calling if we disregard the law of love. It's like the runner who reaches the finish line only to discover he's been disqualified for cutting in on his fellow runner. He was running very well but at the expense of his fellow athlete. So when the medals are given out, he'll have to be among the spectators as though he never even run. That's how our spiritual race in life is. We are to run it in such a way as to gain the heavenly prize without being a hindrance or stumbling block to others. We mustn't be guilty of causing others to turn away from Jesus or to refuse to accept Him. We must stay in our lane and let others be encouraged to run their race because of our example.

How we relate to one another is of paramount importance in our quest for the heavenly prize. Unlike the Olympiads, we are not competing against one another but are following the example of the Greatest Champion of All Time – Jesus Christ our Lord. He is the One Who overcame and sat on the Father's throne and invites us to do the same. He will reward those who overcome as He overcame. He wants us to be champions patterned after Him. But the only way we can do it is by following His example of laying down His life for others in faithful service to the Father. This love that lays down its rights in order to serve others is what will cause us to reach our high calling in God. It is the love from which nothing in all creation can separate us. Its origin is not natural but divine. This is the love that should make the whole world realize that we are Christ's disciples. I believe it's our greatest witness to the world and will attract them to Christ more than anything else will.

How You Treat People

So if we are to reach our high calling in Christ we need to pass what I call "The People Test." This has to do essentially with how we treat people and is second only to how we treat God. I don't know what you will say when Jesus asks you: "How did you treat the people that you lived with, worked with, or met each day of your life?" I hope to have a good answer that day. I surely want to be among those who lived a life of love to the glory of God.

The golden rule could very well qualify you for a golden crown. This powerful rule could be restated as follows: Treat people the way you want people to treat you. Some people may think this is hard but it's not so hard when you truly understand and experience God's love for you. It is only when His love overwhelms you that you can love others the way God loves them. His love will make you act compassionately towards those you wouldn't otherwise love. It will make you love those who criticize and gossip about you. It will cause you to overcome any relationship problem you may ever face. It will motivate you to pray for those who mistreat you and cause you to treat them better than they deserve. Your good treatment of others will, to a large extent, determine your position in eternity.

The golden rule could very well qualify you for a golden crown.

Treating other people like dirt will cost you greatly on that day. If you think you can just use people like little puppets and treat them any way you feel like, then you've got something else coming! The bible says we will be judged the same way we judge others. I believe this means if we condemn others, we will reap condemnation in this life and lose rewards at the judgment.

But by the same token, if we show others mercy, we too will be shown mercy by others in this life and reap rewards at the judgment. Remember, mercy triumphs over judgment! (James 2:13).That was what the Apostle John also talked about in 1 John 4:16-18: *"And so we know and rely on the love God has for us. God is love. Whoever lives in love lives in God, and God in him. In this way, love is made complete among us so that we will have confidence on the Day of Judgment, because in this world we are like Him. There is no fear in love. But perfect love drives out fear, because fear has to do with punishment. The one who fears is not made perfect in love."* It's encouraging to know that you can live in such a way as to be confident when you stand before the Lord on that day. It's His love that will make us confident to stand before Him. So as much as the message of the Judgment Seat of Christ should shake us up to be serious, it should also make us realize how vitally important it is to walk in the love of God.

Now, here is something we need to understand about God if we are to have a balanced view of Him. God is a God of love as well as judgment. If you look at Jesus, you can see both a loving Savior and a Righteous Judge. He is both the Lion and the Lamb. He has a soft side as well as a tough side. Even the revelation of God as Father shows us that He cares tenderly for us and disciplines those He loves. We must *"consider therefore the kindness and sternness of God..."* (Romans 11:22). This means that we should have a deep respect for God and all that pertains to Him which includes the people that He created in His own image. This also means that we should understand how much He loves us in order for us to love like Him.

People for Ministry or Ministry for People

The Son of man did not come to be served but to serve (Mark 10:45). He set us an example of what true ministry really is. It is only when we do our service unselfishly for His glory that we will truly impact eternity. If our ministry is not based on love for God and people, them I'm afraid our works will burn to ashes.

Ministry was made to serve people, and every born again Christian has a ministry of some kind besides the ministry of reconciliation (bringing people to Christ). Yet sometimes it seems as if ministry itself is the issue and that people are simply a part of the ministry and that life revolves around ministry. But the bible shows us that people are the ones who are the focus of His love and that ministry is simply a way to show people that love. So to make ministry our focus and to use people as ministry resources is to reverse the order. We need to focus on reaching people and use ministry as a means to do so. Let us not fall into the trap of using people simply to make "our" ministry big and successful while treating them as mere resources to achieve "our" vision. It is not the people who are supposed to be making our ministry big. It is our ministry that should be helping them to grow big in God. Your ministry exists to serve people. Not the other way around.

People are not just resources to be classified together with money, materials and machines. They are not merely resources you can use. No. They are special. They are created in God's image after His likeness. I, personally, am not pleased with the phrase 'human resource' even though I believe people should be resourceful. I don't believe people should be viewed the same way you view money or machines. I believe this view encourages the use of people as work horses. It makes us want to use them for our purposes. But God wants us to see how best we can be a blessing to people, how we can use our gifts, talents, finances, and influence to help them become what God designed them to be.

God wants us to go beyond just seeing crowds to identifying individuals who we can help. He wants us to reach out to a person and treat them special with the love of God. Crowds are great but it's high time we took time to know individual people and listen long enough to what they have to say so that we can be more relevant to their needs. I'm not against crowds but I think we need to be reaching individuals who are hurting out there. We need to go to the single moms, the widows, the orphans and the homeless. You may not touch the whole world alone, but if each one of us ministered to the individuals that God brings our way, surely our collective impact would be astronomical.

So you see, it's not about being the biggest anything, it's about serving others with a heart of love as unto the Lord. That's the true essence of ministry. Now, of course, people can participate in your ministry but the goal must not be to use them simply to build your ministry. Rather you should use your ministry to build the people. You should help them fulfill their ministry as they help you fulfill yours. That way the body of Christ will grow mutually into a giant in the earth.

How Did You Use Your Influence?

Whether you realize it or not, you are in one way or another influencing someone. Your life is a book being read by people you come in contact with. The bible calls Christians the living epistles or letters of Christ. Our conduct or behavior is to be a witness to those around us. How we conduct ourselves at work, at school, at home, and everywhere else we go has a bearing on whether someone will stumble or stand. It has a bearing on whether people will shun the gospel or accept it. This influence through our example is bound to affect our reward in eternity.

For example, as a parent, how you influence your children today can determine whether or not they make Jesus their Lord. It could determine whether or not they grow up to become the people God ordained them to be. This shows us that parenting is a far greater responsibility than secular society has taught us. It has more far-reaching consequences than we can imagine. It is one of the greatest ways to perpetuate godliness in the earth. That is the very essence of parenthood. We are called to raise children in the ways of the Lord. God, in His word clearly points out this most awesome responsibility of a father and mother. *"Has not the Lord made them one? In flesh and spirit they are his. And why one? Because he was seeking godly offspring. So guard yourself in your spirit, and do not break faith with the wife of your youth"* (Malachi 2:15). So, it's not a matter of having children anyhow. It's a matter of raising a generation of godly people who will do exploits for the Lord.

God wants our children to go farther than us in fulfilling His purposes. He wants each generation to provide a solid faith foundation for the next. That is one sure way righteousness can be perpetuated in the earth. That, my friends, is the power of influence over our children. In fact, I dare say that if you have no intention of raising godly offspring who will serve God, then don't have children.

So parents, especially housewives, may you be encouraged. Just because you don't have a worldwide prophetic or teaching ministry like so-and-so, does not mean what you are doing for the Lord is less important. That child you are raising could be your greatest reward. Just faithfully teach that child the word of God, pray for and with them, take them to children's church, teach them good Christian conduct, and God will credit you with all that that child will accomplish when they grow up. It may be that that child will do such mighty exploits to where millions will come to know the Lord all because you faithfully prayed and raised them in the fear of the Lord. Then guess who will be the first to share the reward for all those souls saved? So don't despise your day of small beginnings. Don't look down on your God-given assignment. Send your children forth beyond where you are and they will reap rewards that you all can share! It's not how popular you are in this world, but how faithful you are that will earn you rewards.

Many of us will be surprised when we get to heaven because some of the people we thought would be the greatest will actually be among the least, while those we thought never achieved anything will be among the top brass. God does not measure greatness the way man does. He looks not just at the deed but also the heart behind the deed. He knows whether we do something out of wanting to impress people or to genuinely help someone and glorify God. True greatness is achieved through love, humility and faithful service. It is only those who know and are known intimately by God who will do the Father's will and thus be considered great in His eyes. Better to humble yourself and let God exalt you, than to be proud and be humiliated. To humble yourself is humility, but to have God humble you is humiliation.

Listen: God hasn't called you to be the biggest or to worry about what others are doing. He just wants you to abide in Him and do His will. It's not about being in the limelight. It's about doing what's right – and that's the Father's will. The right thing for you to do is the purpose for which you were created. Find it out and do it with all your heart. Your reward depends on it! Live in such a way that your daily conduct will win the interest of those who don't know Christ. Let your lifestyle as well as your words preach to them. You are salt and light to influence your community for Christ.

Integrity and Hypocrisy

Are you a man or woman of your word? Do you say what you truly mean and mean what you say? If what you say and what you do don't properly line up, then you're lacking something called integrity. People of integrity are not promise breakers. They are people who keep their word even when it hurts.

When we stand before the Lord, we will be examined for our integrity or the lack of it. Idle words spoken will have to be accounted for. That means unfulfilled pledges and promises we made could cost us dearly. Do any of them come to mind? Folks, we must truly repent from the heart and make a quality decision to live a life of integrity in Christ. We must become blameless and pure before Him in love.

The Lord has a recording angel at your side, recording every conversation you make. He is documenting every word you utter to yourself, to God and to other people. He is compiling your record of words to be opened on that day. I'm not saying this to frighten you but to help you think seriously about your words. You need to realize that God places a high premium on words.

It's no joke. Your words – together with your motives and actions - will determine your heavenly rewards.

Consider carefully what you say from day to day. I'm examining myself as well. I'm praying to be a man of integrity who does not make false promises but follows through on every word I say, knowing it will count on that day. I want to be able to keep my word like God keeps His. It's better to say no to someone than say yes and not follow through. We must get to a place where our words are trustworthy and reliable if we ever hope to fare well on that day. We have to be men and women of integrity. Please take the time to read Psalm 15 to get a clear picture of what integrity is all about.

Practice What You Preach

> *"...for they do not practice what they preach"* (Matthew 23:3b).

It is dangerous to preach what you do not practice. It's like the "financial expert" who tells everybody else how to handle their finances when he himself is on the verge of bankruptcy due to poor financial management. How can you be a "marriage expert" who teaches others how to build healthy marriages when your own marriage is in shambles? It's called "the blind leading the blind." It's not just preachers, but anyone who requires others to do what he himself is not willing to do or has never done before. If you instruct others to forgive and love, do you practice that yourself? If you teach others anything from the Word, are you sure you have personally proven what you are recommending to others?

You see, Jesus never just preached. He lived the life He proclaimed to others. He was the message He preached. That's integrity. That is how God expects us to live. We are to be living epistles of the message we proclaim. Integrity is living your life as an open book. You don't have anything to hide.

134

Now James tells us that those who teach will be judged more strictly (James 3:1). I believe that's because they are more likely than anyone to lead masses of people astray with wrong teaching. Secondly, they are more likely to fall into the trap of teaching others what they themselves do not practice, which amounts to hypocrisy. Yet on the other hand, those who do preach the truth in love and live the message they preach will lead many to know the Lord and do God's will for their lives. Thus their eternal reward will be great as Daniel 12:3 (AMP) reveals:

> "And the teachers and those who are wise shall shine like the brightness of the firmament, and those who turn many to righteousness, to uprightness and rightstanding with God) [shall give forth light] like the stars forever and ever."

'Go Tell My People I Am Coming'

> "Behold, I am coming soon! My reward is with me, and I will give to everyone according to what he has done" (Revelation 22:12).

I will never forget listening to Evangelist Jesse Duplantis' inspiring testimony from his sermon entitled *Heaven – Close Encounters of The God-Kind*. In it he narrates how he got caught up in the Spirit to heaven for over five hours to among other things receive a message for the church. So he gets to meet Jesus and the Lord says to him, "Go tell my people I am coming." Jesse replies to the Lord, "But they already know that." The Lord says, "No, they don't. Go tell them I'm coming."

I know some people don't believe in supernatural experiences of this nature but the Bible does say that in the last days God will pour out His Spirit on all flesh and the result will be visions, dreams and prophecy (Acts 2:16-18) Experiences of being caught up to heaven like Jesse had should come as no surprise to the Spirit-filled believer. Paul speaks of just such an experience in 1 Corinthians 12:1-4 where he was caught up to the third heaven. John the revelator also had a supernatural experience of being caught up to heaven in the Spirit as is evidenced in the book of Revelation.

But what is important is to examine these supernatural revelations and visions in the light of the Holy Scriptures. If they agree with scripture, then we can accept them as coming from God. But if they don't, we can dismiss them. However, in examining Jesse's testimony, I have found it to be both scripturally sound and edifying. I believe its message is of vital importance to the end time church. We must take heed to its message to help us prepare for His soon return. The underlying message is: **we must live rapture-ready everyday**.

I refuse to rest until I get this radical message across to people: **Jesus Christ is coming soon and you must be prepared to meet Him at His coming**. If you know what it takes to prepare for His return and do it, you will rejoice on that day. But if you don't, chances are that you will be caught unaware. Let us live in such a way that we will not be ashamed when He appears. Ladies and gentlemen, be warned. The rapture is not for every Jim and Jack. It is only for those that long for and love His appearing.

I feel sad when I hear people downplay the message of His return. They say something like, *"Let's focus on what affects us now and not so much on the future."* They fail to realize that this message greatly affects how we live today. It is one of the greatest incentives for living our lives to the fullest. It adds that extra spring in our step, just like an upcoming exam will motivate a student to study harder.

It's amazing how even the Holy Communion speaks of the death of our Lord on the cross in relation to His return for His saints. We are to reflect on what Jesus did for us on Calvary's cross and anticipate His soon return. That is the reason for Holy Communion. *"For whenever you eat this bread and drink this cup, you proclaim the Lord's death until He comes"* (1

Corinthians 11:26). The return of the Lord is a part of our great redemption in Christ. In fact it is the completion or consummation of our great redemption when our bodies are glorified. How can you not look forward to that?

There is not a more exciting event to look forward to than the return of our Lord Jesus Christ to get His bride. We have been left here on earth to dress up for our wedding day. We need to adorn ourselves with holiness, love and purity expecting to be whisked away at a moment's notice. Always remember one thing; Jesus will fulfill His promise to His bride: *"...I will come back and take you to be with me that you also may be where I am"* (John 14:3). That's our hope, saints. That's our blessed hope!

The last words of Jesus in the Bible are, "Yes, I am coming soon" (Revelation 22:20). These words are supposed to fill us with anticipation each moment of every day. They should give us extra motivation for fulfilling His will for our lives. We should be like Moses who forsook the pleasures of sin and other earthly pursuits "because he was looking ahead to his reward" (Hebrews 11:26). He wasn't focused on making earthly history. He wanted his story to be inscribed on the pages of eternity. So just like Moses, we too should fix our eyes on Jesus, the Author and Finisher of our faith as we run our spiritual race here on earth. We must hear the heavenly host say, "Run, Church, run and hasten the day of His coming!" Can you hear the people in heaven cheering and screaming your name? "Go on! Don't give up!" they say. They have already run their race and are sitting in the grandstands of heaven wanting you to finish yours. Are you going to disappoint them? Are you going to make the whole stadium go "Oh!" Or you are going to keep them on the edge of their seats as you fulfill their hope of a victorious end time church! The choice is yours. Make every effort to run and finish your course with joy. Run, run, and run!

Listen again: the Lord's coming is very soon. Jesus is coming back very soon. It may be sooner than you think! Don't waste your life on earth. Use it to the fullest in service to Him. We must be about our Father's business like never before! Seek first the kingdom of God and His righteousness and all other things shall be added to you as well (Matthew 6:33). You must put your priorities in order by placing spiritual things first. It is sad that some of us believers and even preachers have lost our enthusiasm for the Lord's return. How would we feel if the people that were supposed to be expecting us in a particular city were not even making preparations for our coming? Would we feel they were ready to receive us? I suppose not. But then how do we suppose Jesus feels about our lack of enthusiasm, coupled with our lack of preparation for His return? It must be heart-breaking, don't you think?

You see, just knowing the fact that Jesus will some day come does not ensure your readiness to meet Him. You must take means and measures to keep yourself prepared at all times. According to the book of Hebrews 9:28, Jesus will only appear to take to heaven those who long for His return. Readiness is not an option. It's a must. You must live each day expecting Him to come. Jesus warned that those who do not live in daily expectation and readiness would be caught unaware. Read and meditate on these two scriptures:

> *"You also must be ready, because the Son of Man will come at an hour when you do not expect him"* (Luke 12:20).

> *"Be careful, or your hearts will be weighed down with dissipation, drunkenness and the anxieties of life, and that day will close on you unexpectedly like a trap"* (Luke 21:34).

Pastors, I urge you to prepare God's people for Christ's return. Warn those who are sleeping to wake up and be spiritually alert. Tell them to watch and pray and do all they know to do in God's word as they look forward to His return. Equip them to fulfill the assignment God has for them. That is your assignment.

For you, church members, your assignment is not any less important than your pastors'. We all have an important part to play in God's grand plan. Every assignment is important. It doesn't matter how small it may look to you, it is still very important. Your reward does not depend on how big or small your ministry is. It depends on how faithful you are with the particular assignment that God has for you.

Many of us will really be surprised when we get to heaven. Some of the most popular Christians on earth will be the least in heaven while those who were unknown but served God faithfully will be the greatest. To be great in God's eyes takes love, humility and faithfulness in service. God exalts the humble and humiliates the proud. We must not think we are greater than others but rather consider others better than ourselves (Philippians 2:3). What a change would occur in the body of Christ if we all had that attitude!

God's best for you is to know Him intimately and to fulfill His will for your life. It's not about being in the limelight where everyone can see you and praise you for your good works. It's about doing everything for the glory of Him whose honor you seek. Do all you do as unto the Lord and you'll discover a great reward at the end of your life. Don't compete with others or compare yourself to them. Just be faithful with God's specific assignment for you. Every kingdom assignment is important. Allow me to illustrate it as follows:

Four groups of people were to provide a meal for a gathering of 100. Each group had a task. Team A was to purchase the food; Team B was to cook the food; Team C was to serve the food; and Team D was to clean the dishes. If these tasks represented God's purposes for our lives, would any task be more or less important than the other? No! Each task is important but the quality of our work will determine our rewards. That's how God's kingdom works. We all have one overall purpose – to extend His Kingdom in the earth – even though our individual tasks are different. That is what Paul talks about in 1 Corinthians 3:6-8: "I planted the seed, Apollos watered it, but God made it grow. So neither he who plants nor he who waters is anything, but only

God, who makes things grow. The man who plants and the man who waters have one purpose, and each will be rewarded according to his own labor." So don't despise your assignment. Do it faithfully to the glory of God and you can be sure of a great reward in heaven!

Staying Rapture-Ready

Allow me to state what I consider to be the two main keys for making it in the rapture.

1. **Faith** – Jesus will appear to those who expect His return. Like I said in the beginning, when the Son of Man returns, He will be looking for faith in the earth. Our faith in the blessed hope will become a reality just like Enoch's faith was instrumental in translating Him from time to eternity. I am a firm believer that the rapture as a redemptive benefit should be appropriated or received by faith. Those who believe that Jesus is coming to get them will most certainly fly up to Him in the clouds when He calls. *"And just as it is appointed for [all] men once to die, and after that the [certain] judgment, Even so it is that Christ, having been offered to take upon Himself and bear as a burden the sins of many once and once for all, will appear a second time, not to carry any burden of sin nor to deal with sin, but to bring to full salvation those who are [eagerly, constantly, and patiently] waiting for and expecting Him."* Hebrews 9:27-28 AMP

2. **Spirit-Filled Living** – The fullness of the Spirit is essential to making it in the rapture. If you look at the lives of Enoch, Elijah and Jesus, you'll discover that they were men who operated in the realm of the Spirit. These men were led by the Spirit of God and were carried to heaven by the same. I do not see how anyone who is not well acquainted with the Holy Spirit will make it in the rapture. The parable of the virgins tells us that only those who carried extra oil – a type of the Holy Spirit – with

their lamps went with the bridegroom while the others remained (Matthew 25:1-13).

Oil is a fuel and I suppose if you don't have enough fuel, your rocket will not take off. Folks, it's imperative that we are continually refilled with the Spirit of God to stay tuned to Him so that when the Lord says, "Come up here!" we will be caught up to meet Him in the air. That is why your prayer life must be in tip-top condition all the time so that you are always full and yielded to the Holy Spirit of God.

CHAPTER 7

A CHRONOLOGY OF WORLD EVENTS

I now want to present to you a brief summary of end time world events as I believe the bible sets them forth. I trust it will help you realize how close we are to the end this age and the beginning of the new one under Christ Jesus our Lord.

But first let me share with you a little bit about how I came to fall in love with end time teaching. It all began when I came across a mini book by Jimmy Swaggart on the rapture of the church. I was so intrigued by the subject that I've never stopped studying it since. I had never known that the rapture was such an important and even major subject. The book spoke about the early days of Jimmy Swaggart's Christian life when he heard much preaching about the coming of the Lord. This lit a fire in my heart that has never stopped burning. I was determined to learn more and be fully prepared to meet the Lord at His coming. The impact that this message has had on my life is worth eternity itself. It is a subject that has put a spring in my step and kept me on the edge of my seat, so to speak. I am living for that day and I pray that as I share these truths, the hope of Christ's return will produce the zeal in you to serve Him faithfully for the remainder of these last few days before the Lord comes. I will echo the words of Jesus in Luke 21:36:

> *"Be always on the watch, and pray that you may be able to escape all that is about to happen, and that you may be able to stand before the Son of Man."*

The Purpose of Bible Prophecy

Have you ever seen a movie trailer and wanted to watch the movie afterwards? Well, the Bible also gives us what we would consider previews of coming attractions. They are called end time events and they are coming to pass on a scale you can hardly believe.

"For the essence of prophecy is to give a clear witness for Jesus" (Revelation 19:10b NLT).

All end time prophecy must testify of Jesus. This is the yardstick for judging whether the teaching is balanced or not. It should inspire faith not fear. It should be a message of hope not despair. Even the warnings it gives should inspire us to prepare, and not to panic. So while the world is in turmoil and despair, the church will experience their finest hour. The day of the army of the Lord has come. It's time to stand up and be counted. May the words from the book of Revelation hold true for what I have endeavored to share with you: *"Blessed is the one who reads the words of this prophecy, and blessed are those who hear it and take to heart what is written in it because the time is near"* (Revelation 1:3).

A lot of people have no idea what is about to transpire on planet earth. They are unaware that things have radically changed and will continue to change in fulfillment of Bible prophecy. We have come to the place where Bible prophecies are coming to pass in quick succession. The end of all things is at hand. We must pray and work like never before.

The Signs of The Times

The signs of the times are upon us and we need to know what they are. *"He replied, When evening comes, you say, It will be fair weather, for the sky is red, and in the morning, Today it will be stormy, for the sky is red and overcast. You know how to interpret the appearance of the sky, but you cannot interpret the signs of the times"* (Matthew 16:2-3). The King James Version actually says, *"...can ye not discern the signs of the times?"*

Interpreting or understanding the times that we are living in is of vital importance if we are to navigate through the storms of the end. The pilot who does not know how to interpret the "appearance of the sky" may be in for a rude shock. Yet the signs of the end are not all negative. There's a positive side as well. The bible says that the time of greatest darkness for the world will be a time of greatest light for the church (Isaiah 60:1-3). The time of economic turmoil for the world will be a time of economic blessing for the church. While the world is experiencing an economic recession, the church will be enjoying an economic progression (Isaiah 60:5). This is the time for the fulfillment of the end-time wealth transfer prophecies in which the wealth of the nations will come into the hands of God's people to fund the greatest harvest of souls ever seen. So it's not all doom and gloom preaching. There're some good days ahead too – for the Church that is - but not for the world. The world is headed for their worst in the course of human history – the great tribulation. But the church will experience its most glorious days just before it's caught up to heaven. We will have a glorious exit from this planet.

In Matthew 24 Jesus gives a detailed forecast of the signs of the times that will lead up to His glorious return. Among the signs Jesus mentions we have:

- Deceivers who claim to represent Christ or even impersonate Christ working great signs and miracles that are of satanic origin. These will lead many people astray. You had better keep your eyes open and discern false ministers by checking out their fruit (character, integrity, and personal history). You will know them by their fruit. Some are even on TV and radio masquerading as ministers of Christ.
- Wars and rumors of wars.
- Ethnic (tribal and racial) conflict.
- Famines whose extended meaning includes all kinds of economic disasters.
- Earthquakes in various places and no doubt we've seen a greater number of earthquakes in recent times than at any other time in history. There is such an upheaval of

nature that climate change has become a major issue on world leaders' forums. "Global warming" is a familiar phrase now.

- Persecution of Christians like never before.
- A falling away from the faith by many who will even betray and hate each other. Let this not be you.
- In Mark 13:12 Jesus says that rebellion against parents will also be one of the signs that will precede His glorious return.
- The increase of wickedness which will result in the love of many growing cold. Paul further elaborates on Christ's teaching in 1 Timothy 4:1-5 and 2 Timothy 3:1-9 which you can read from your own bible.
- The preaching of the gospel of the kingdom to the whole world before the end comes. In fact this preaching will be continued by some of the tribulation saints together with the 144,000 Jewish evangelists who will be specially selected and sealed by God. I must say that even if worldwide evangelism appears as one of the signs, it is more than just a sign. It is both a proclamation and a demonstration of the rule of God all over the world. It is the witness of His return. In fact it is the number one thing on God's agenda. And once this gospel has reached the ends of the earth, you can rest assured the Lord shall appear. So let's speed up His coming by preaching the gospel to sinners around us.

The Rapture of the Church

The next event on God's agenda following the global harvest of souls is the rapture of the church. The major reason why the rapture hasn't occurred yet is because God wants to give opportunity to more people to repent. Peter tells us that in these last days scoffers will come saying *"where is this coming that He promised"* (2 Peter 3:4). But then Peter points us to the reason why the Lord will have tarried His coming. He says in 2 Peter 3:9 that *"The Lord is not slow in keeping his promise, as some understand slowness. He is patient with you, not wanting anyone to perish, but everyone to come to repentance."* So that is why Jesus has tarried His coming. But be sure of this one thing: He is coming anytime from now to take to heaven all the prepared saints. So get yourself ready and invite as many people as you can to go with you to heaven.

The Judgment Seat of Christ

Jesus will carry the believers who are ready to heaven to appear before His judgment seat so that He can give each one the reward that is due to them. *"For we must all appear and be revealed as we are before the Judgment Seat of Christ, so that each may receive [his pay] according to what he has done in the body, whether good or evil [considering what his purpose and motive have been, and what he has achieved, been busy with, and given himself and his attention to accomplishing]."* (1 Corinthians 5:10) This rewards ceremony will be taking place in heaven while the world is in a state of chaos.

The Lord Jesus will examine and evaluate our work which we did while on earth to determine what reward we will get. Some will receive a full reward, others a partial reward, while still others no reward at all. The eternal rewards that will be given will include kingly positions on glorious thrones, crowns, territories to rule over, and many other indescribable privileges and responsibilities in God's eternal kingdom. *"Now if any man build upon this foundation gold, silver, precious stones, wood, hay, stubble; Every man's work shall be made manifest: for the day shall declare it, because it shall be revealed by fire; and the fire shall try every man's work of what sort it is. If any man's work abide which he built thereupon, he shall receive a reward. If any man's work shall be burned, he shall suffer loss: but he himself shall be saved; yet so as by fire."* 1 Corinthians 3:12-15

The Marriage Supper of the Lamb

Once the rewards ceremony is over and the rewarded believers are fully dressed in their royal attire with robes and crowns, it will now be time for the most glorious wedding ceremony of all time. This royal wedding, like the rewards ceremony, also takes place in heaven while the tribulation on earth is at its peak. The

Bridegroom (Jesus Christ) and His eternal Bride (believers from every generation) will be joined in the holiest of matrimonies at the Father's throne.

We will then sit to dine at the Lord's Table and enjoy fellowship with our Bridegroom and with one another. Speaking of this most anticipated of events, Jesus Himself said, *"I say to you, that many will come from the east and the west, and will take their places at the feast with Abraham, Isaac, and Jacob in the kingdom of heaven."* (Matthew 8:11) The most intimate honeymoon on earth is a fleeting fantasy compared to the eternal and most intimate honeymoon of this heavenly couple. Nothing will ever disturb or interrupt our intimacy with Him. The Old Testament believers and their New Testament counterparts will all be gathered to enjoy this great celebration feast. The Book of Revelation puts in this way:

> *"Let us rejoice and shout for joy [exulting and triumphant]! Let us celebrate and ascribe to Him glory and honor, for the marriage of the Lamb [at last] has come, and His bride has prepared herself.*

> *She has been permitted to dress in fine (radiant) linen, dazzling and white – for the fine linen is (signifies, represents) the righteousness (the upright just and godly living, deeds and conduct, and right standing with God) of the saints (God's holy people).*

> *Then [the angel] said to me, Write this down: Blessed (happy, to be envied) are those who are summoned (invited, called) to the marriage supper of the Lamb. And he said to me [further], These are the true words (the genuine and exact declarations) of God."* Revelation 19:7-9 AMP

The Tribulation Begins

The rapture of the church will signal the beginning of the seven year tribulation period that the bible talks about. It will be a time of trouble comparable to no other in the history of man. First and foremost, when the rapture happens, there will inevitably be untold chaos all over the world. How else could it be since Christian pilots, drivers, and machine operators will have all disappeared while on the job? Can you imagine what will happen to houses whose appliances like stoves will have been left on when the rapture happens. I can see fires, accidents, and plane crashes all over the world. And what do you suppose the news will look like? I mean for months it will be one headline after another. Just that initial chaos will be enough to cause more than enough panic and fear for a world leader to very easily assume the reins of power by giving people a false hope that will lead them to destruction. I can imagine a heads of state summit quickly convened to try to bring order in the whole world. Then from among the world leaders one man is chosen and endorsed perhaps by the UN and other world organizations to chart the way forward for the whole world. This leader that is chosen becomes the Antichrist that the Bible says will emerge at the end of days.

Antichrist and the False Prophet

The Antichrist will not show his true colors at first but will come as a man of peace and will appear to be very diplomatic. He will seek to bring peace to the world through expert diplomatic tactics. The world will be amazed at how he will accomplish the seemingly impossible namely the signing of a historic seven-year peace treaty between Israel and the Palestinians which will end the hostility between the two parties for a while. The world will stand in awe of this great 'prince of peace' who is trying to imitate the real Prince of Peace, Jesus Christ. He will probably get the Nobel Peace Prize for such a milestone achievement. The bible calls him *"a stern-faced king, a master of intrigue"* (Daniel 8:23). In other words he is a diplomatic mastermind who will deceive like no politician ever has. In fact, that is how he will rise to power - through peace not war. *"He will cause deceit to prosper, and he will consider himself superior. When they feel secure, he will destroy many and take his stand against the*

Prince of princes. Yet he will be destroyed, but not by human power" (Daniel 8:25).

He will give the Jews freedom to build their own temple so that they can restore their ancient sacrificial system like it was in the bible days. Won't this make many of them believe he's the messiah they've been waiting for? They will enjoy peace through that covenant or treaty for only the first half of the seven years and that's when the unthinkable will happen.

The Antichrist will break that treaty with them and persecute them. He will take off his sheep's skin and be seen for what he is – a wolf! He will introduce a new order or system of doing things politically, economically and religiously. Daniel 7:25 says, *"He will speak against the Most High and oppress his saints and try to change the set times and the laws. The saints will be handed over to him for a time, times and half a time."* That means for a period of three and a half years which is the second half of the seven year tribulation. The saints that he will oppress are those left behind after the rapture.

This man known as the Antichrist will among other things be:

- A great politician and diplomat
- A very persuasive orator or public speaker
- A military genius
- An expert at economics, and
- A very religious man

His intention is to establish:

- A one world government
- A one world economy, and
- A one world religion

Then somewhere along the line he will introduce his special agent known as the False Prophet. This man will perform *"great* and miraculous signs, even causing fire to come down from heaven to earth in full view of men" (Revelation 13:13). He will use these satanic miracles to deceive and force many to bow down and worship the Antichrist and his idolatrous image. Those who refuse to worship will be killed. He will also force men and women to receive the mark of the beast without which they will not be able to buy or sell. He will be the Antichrist's right hand man – the religious leader of the world. These two demon-possessed individuals will wreck much havoc in the earth. They will be the ultimate expression of man's depravity due to sin.

The 144,000 Jewish Evangelists

Yet right in the middle of the tribulation we see the 144,000 Jewish evangelists being appointed to preach the gospel to every creature. I believe they will be proclaiming the message of the coming kingdom of our God and of His Christ and will lead a great multitude of people to the Lord. They will preach without the Antichrist stopping or hindering them because they will be specially protected by God. They will fulfill their assignment and be taken to heaven by Christ. The bible says, *"They follow the Lamb wherever He goes..."* (Revelation 14:4).

The Tribulation Saints

Many people will turn to Christ during the tribulation as a result of the preaching of the 144,000 Jewish evangelists. It seems reasonable that many unprepared Christians who were left behind at the time of the rapture will also fully commit themselves to Christ. These believers in Christ will make up what we call the tribulation saints and will be composed of both Jews and Gentiles. They are the ones who will face the greatest persecution to ever occur on this planet. Many of them will die as martyrs for Jesus. The Antichrist and his wicked followers will behead great numbers of believers at that time. I believe these are some of the saints whose souls John saw in heaven as follows:

"When he opened the fifth seal, I saw under the altar the souls of those who had been slain because of the word of God and the testimony they had maintained. They called out in a loud voice, How long, Sovereign Lord, holy and true, until you judge the inhabitants of the earth and avenge our blood? Then each of them was given a white robe, and they were told to wait a little longer, until the number of their fellow-servants and brothers who were to be killed as they had been was completed." (Revelation 6:9)

Yet in spite of the mass killings of believers during that time, there will also be a great number of tribulation saints who will not only survive the tribulation, but will actually thrive during that period. It is amazing just how much more God's grace will abound during that time over and above the great difficulties.

At the very time when the idolatrous image of the beast (the abomination that causes desolation) is introduced for worldwide worship, and people are forced to bow, the tribulation saints will stand up tall for Christ like Shadrach, Meshach and Abednego of old. They will resist the Antichrist and do great things for God. Speaking of the time when the tribulation will have reached its height this is what the Bible says:

"His armed forces will rise up to desecrate the temple fortress and will abolish the daily sacrifice. Then they will set up the abomination that causes desolation. With flattery he will corrupt those who have violated the covenant, but the people who know their God will firmly resist him. Those who are wise will instruct many though for a time they will fall by the sword or be burned or captured or plundered. When they fall, they will receive a little help, and many who are not sincere will join them. Some of the wise will stumble, so that they may be refined, purified and made spotless until the time of the end, for it will still come at the appointed time." (Daniel 11:31-35)

It's a blessing to know that the tribulation saints who know their God will take their stand and resist the Antichrist. The Amplified Bible puts it this way: *"but the people who know their God shall prove themselves strong and shall stand firm and do exploits [for God]."* Daniel 11:32b The time of *great* tribulation will also be a time of *great* exploits for God! The proclamation of God's kingdom and the teaching of His word will continue to prevail. The ministry of the Holy Spirit and that of His angels will be very active during that time. The tribulation saints, just like their counterparts who went in the rapture, will eventually be presented to Christ as *"a radiant church, without spot or wrinkle or any other blemish, but holy and blameless."* (Ephesians 5:27)

So the tribulation is not just full of doom, gloom and darkness. It is also filled with victory, hope and glory. Many of the tribulation saints will be alive to witness the glorious return of Jesus to reign on the earth. They'll be the welcome party, so to speak. At that time this is what the Bible says will happen: *"Then the sovereignty, power and greatness of the kingdoms under the whole heaven will be handed over to the saints, the people of the Most High. His kingdom will be an everlasting kingdom, and all rulers will worship and obey him."* Daniel 7:17 Now that's a triumphant end to a victorious life any way you look at it!

The Time of Great Tribulation

The Antichrist and the False Prophet will institute a system of capital punishment for those who refuse to comply with their demands. They will especially persecute and kill those who believe in the true Messiah - Jesus Christ. Those who will refuse to join their satanic worship will be beheaded. There will be distress such as never has been since man first set foot on this planet.

But then the Antichrist will not be victorious over everyone. For there will be some who will overcome the trials and tribulations of that time. I believe that God's grace will be even more pronounced during that time for *"where sin abounded, grace did much more abound"* (Romans 5:20 KJV). The Bible tells us that during the time of the great tribulation, there will be an army of saints who will do great things for God's kingdom. *"And such as do wickedly against the covenant shall he corrupt by flatteries: but the people that do know their God shall be strong, and do exploits"* (Daniel 11:32 KJV). These tribulation saints together with the 144,000 Jewish Evangelists and the two witnesses, will proclaim the gospel of the kingdom to all nations until the day Jesus returns to set up His glorious millennial reign.

The bible in Revelation says, *"And I saw what looked like a sea of glass mixed with fire and, standing beside the sea, those who had been victorious over the beast and his image and over the number of his name. They held harps given them by God"* (Revelation15:2). Based on the scriptures we've just read, I believe the saints will be victorious over the beast in two ways. Firstly, there will be those who will overcome him by laying down their lives as martyrs for Jesus because they refused to worship the beast or accept his mark. They will glorify God by demonstrating that they love Him more than their very own lives. These will have been faithful to the point of death. They are like the other faith heroes in Hebrews 11 who laid down their lives because they wanted a better resurrection.

The other group of overcomers will be those who, like Shadrach, Meshach and Abednego of old, will overcome the beast without having to die. They will experience God's miraculous protection and deliverance during the most dangerous of times. These will survive the tribulation while proclaiming the kingdom message until the end.

The economic collapse that will ensue will be nothing short of catastrophic, not to mention the wars, natural disasters and such an upheaval of nature that wild animals will start attacking people relentlessly (Revelation 6:8). Great famines and outbreaks of diseases will be widespread as is always the case during wars. There will be death like you never saw; bloodshed like no horror movie can depict. Men's hearts will actually be failing them because of the overwhelming anxiety due to the things that are coming on the earth. But thank God that His mercy will still be at work to save many who will turn to Him during that time.

The Two Witnesses

At the mid point of the seven year tribulation, God will empower His two witnesses to prophecy for 1,260 days dressed in sackcloth. They will be given extraordinary miraculous ability to cause fire to come from their mouths to devour anyone who tries to harm them. They will even have power to stop the rains when they are prophesying and to turn waters into blood not to mention striking the earth with every kind of plague as often as they will. In other words they will pronounce divine judgments when necessary.

The Bible tells us in Revelation 11:7 that the Beast or Antichrist will eventually attack and kill them and leave their bodies on the streets for everyone to see. There will be a public outcry to not have them buried but displayed as conquered foes. The bible tells us that for three and a half days men of all nations will gaze on their bodies and even celebrate their death by sending each other gifts because their tormentors are now gone. I can imagine all major news networks reporting on this event for three and a half days and saying, "The terrorists have finally been killed!" No doubt they will be considered terrorists by the Antichrist's world government.

Now let's read from the book of Revelation to see what happens next. *"But after the three and a half days a breath from God entered them, and they stood on their feet, and terror struck those who saw them. Then they heard a loud voice from heaven saying to them, "Come up here." And they went up to heaven in a cloud, while their enemies looked on"* (Revelation 11:11-12).

Now, mind you, all this will more than likely be shown on live television by the leading news networks of the world. It will be one of the most astonishing sights to behold as their celebration comes to an abrupt end. But that's not all. *"At that very hour there was a severe earthquake and a tenth of the city collapsed. Seven thousand people were killed in the earthquake, and the survivors were terrified and gave glory to the God of heaven"*

(Revelation 11:13). What a triumphant end to their story! The Lord will turn around their cruel and shameful death into one of the most spectacular miraculous wonders the world has ever seen. I have no doubt that many will turn to the Lord after this. So we can see that God will be actively fulfilling His great purposes during the tribulation and will demonstrate His greatness in the earth. Glory to His name!

That is why when you read the book of Revelation or the other biblical books that speak of the end of days, your focus should be more on what God is doing and not so much on what Satan and his cohorts are up to. The purpose of end time prophecy like I've said before is to give a clear witness about Jesus Christ and not the Antichrist. Yes, you need to know certain facts about the Antichrist but only through the eyes of the Christ. **You need to see end-time teaching as a revelation of the glorified King of kings and His great and marvelous purposes. It is a message of hope and victory, not gloom and defeat.**

The Return of Christ

The grandest act of the book of Revelation is the glorious appearing of Christ Jesus with His Church to destroy the Antichrist and his armies and to set up His one thousand year reign. I will try as best as I can to portray a graphic picture of how this momentous event will take place.

The Bible reveals to us that during the seven year tribulation, the saints who had been raptured will be in heaven receiving rewards after which they will celebrate the Marriage Supper of the Lamb. They will also be viewing the events on earth from up above as Revelation 6 shows us. The tribulation will have reached its most critical stage with the Antichrist and his international alliance of armies invading Israel and getting ready to make war against the Lord Jesus Christ. Zechariah picks up on this and tells us exactly what will be happening:

"I will gather all the nations to Jerusalem to fight against it; the city will be captured, the houses ransacked, and the women raped. Half the city will go into exile, but the rest of the people will not be taken from the city. Then the Lord will go out and fight against those nations, as he fights in the day of battle. On that day his feet will stand on the Mount of Olives, east of Jerusalem, and the Mount of Olives will split in two from east to west, forming a great valley...Then the Lord my God will come, and all the holy ones with Him. On that day there will be no light, no cold or frost. It will be a unique day known to the Lord. When evening comes, there will be light. This is the plague with which the Lord will strike all the nations that fought against Jerusalem: Their flesh will rot while they are still standing on their feet, their eyes will rot in their sockets, and their tongues will rot in their mouths. On that day men will be stricken by the Lord with great panic. Each man will seize the hand of another, and they will attack each other. Judah too will fight at Jerusalem. The wealth of all the surrounding nations will be collected – great quantities of gold and silver and clothing...Then the survivors from all the nations that have attacked Jerusalem will go up year after year to worship the King, the Lord Almighty, and to celebrate the Feast of Tabernacles" (Zechariah 14:2-7, 12-14, 16).

This is the most elaborate description or narration of the battle of Armageddon you can find in the bible. So you can readily see that the battle of Armageddon is a full scale war between heavenly and earthly forces and not just a brief conflict. The Lord's appearance in the sky will be sudden and magnificent. I have no doubt that the antichrist and his armies will try to use whatever nuclear weapons they have at the time to fight this "alien invasion." They will try to resist Christ's takeover of the earth. All the nations of the earth will mourn when they see the Son of Man coming on the clouds of the sky with power and great glory (Matthew 24:30). This is indeed when every eye shall see Him. This is when the sun will be darkened and the moon will refuse to shine. The bible also reports that the stars will fall from the sky and the heavenly bodies will be shaken (Mark 13:24-25). The angels of God and the saints will also appear with

Him in glory. They will be dressed ready for battle, riding majestically on white horses. Then right at the coming of the Lord there will be an earthquake so great and violent that *"No earthquake like it has ever occurred since man has been on earth, so tremendous was the quake"* (Revelation 16:18).

You can rest assured that Jesus brings this battle to a decisive end. He's the hero in all this. The Bible says, *"Then I saw the beast and the kings of the earth and their armies gathered together to make war against the rider on the horse and his army. But the Beast was captured, and with him the False Prophet who had performed the miraculous signs on his behalf...The two of them were thrown alive into the fiery lake of burning sulfur. The rest of them were killed with the sword that came out of the mouth of the rider on the horse, and all the birds gorged themselves on their flesh"* (Revelation 19:19-21).

Satan's Arrest and Imprisonment

> *"And I saw an angel coming down out of heaven, having the key to the Abyss and holding in his hand a great chain. He seized the dragon, that ancient serpent, who is the devil, or Satan, and bound him for a thousand years. He threw him into the Abyss, and locked and sealed it over him, to keep him from deceiving the nations any more until the thousand years were ended. After that, he must be set free for a short time."* (Revelation 20:1-3)

At the return of Christ, an angel comes from heaven with a great chain and the key to the Abyss also known as the Bottomless Pit, who seizes Satan and binds and locks him up for a thousand years. He actually throws him into the bottomless pit, locks and seals it so that he cannot deceive the nations until the thousand years are ended. This account of Satan's arrest and imprisonment is just a summary statement. Actually, Satan's fallen angels and demons will all be imprisoned together with him. There will be no evil spirit present during the millennial reign of Christ. That is great news in itself!

157

"How you have fallen from heaven, O morning star, son of the dawn! You have been cast down to the earth, you who once laid low the nations!

But you are brought down to the grave, to the depths of the pit.

Those who see you stare at you, they ponder your fate: Is this the man who shook the earth and made kingdoms tremble, the man who made the world a desert, who overthrew its cities and would not let his captives go home?" (Isaiah 14:12, 15, 17)

The Bible here says that during the millennial reign, people will be able to see Satan in his prison and be amazed that such an insignificant looking fellow could cause such havoc. People will be amazed to see just how small and powerless he is. But blessed are those that see him so now!

The Judgment of the Nations and Israel

Then after Satan's arrest and imprisonment, the Lord will send out angels to bring the nations before Him for judgment. This will be a judgment to determine who of the tribulation survivors will be counted worthy to be part of the millennial kingdom of Christ. It will not be based so much on whether they received Christ or not, but on how they treated the least of Christ's brethren who I believe to be the Jewish people and Christian believers during the tribulation.

The bible says, *"When the Son of Man comes in His glory, and all the angels with Him, He will sit on His throne in heavenly glory. All the nations will be gathered before Him, and He will separate the people one from another as a shepherd separates the sheep from the goats. He will put the sheep on His right and the goats on His left"* (Matthew 25:31-33). From then on you read how that the King will welcome those on His right into the millennial kingdom and turn the nations or people groups on His left into the eternal fire prepared for the devil and his angels.

But like I said earlier, the Judgment of Israel takes place either before or right after the Judgment of the Nations. The Israelites will actually have a national repentance where they will mourn for the one they pierced (Zechariah 12:10-14). This will be the fulfillment of the prophecy that declares that all Israel shall be saved (Romans 11:26-27). These judgments will take place in Israel and pave the way for the millennial reign to begin.

The Millennial Reign of Christ

The millennial reign of Christ is a 1000 year period when Christ and His glorified saints will rule over the Earth in great peace and prosperity. At that time, Jesus will perform a marvelous miracle of raising from the dead those who had been killed for their faith in Him during the tribulation. *"...They came to life and reigned with Christ a thousand years"* (Revelation 20:4). This resurrection is only for the believers who died in the tribulation whereas the wicked dead will only be raised after the millennial reign at the time of the Great White Throne Judgment.

So then, what will really happen during the millennial reign of Christ? Jesus Christ will be King over all the earth reigning from His glorious throne in the city of Jerusalem in Israel (Micah 4:7; Luke 1:31-33). The kingdoms of this world will all become the kingdom of our God and of His Anointed One. There will be a perfect spiritual, social, political and economic system in the earth. With Jesus as King, all the problems which we know today such as poverty, homelessness, disease, crime, wars, and even natural disasters will be eliminated. The peace and love of the Father will prevail over all the earth as the waters cover the sea. Jesus will be personally present and living with us on this earth. The nation of Israel will become the greatest nation on the Earth and Jerusalem will be the seat of Christ's world government. Jerusalem will actually be the capital city of the entire world kingdom of Christ (Micah 4:1-8).

People will trek to Jerusalem to bring Christ gifts, to worship Him and to learn His ways (Zechariah 14:16-21). The ministries of preaching, teaching, writing, singing and many others that we know today will continue in the millennium. If you are a bible teacher, you will still be teaching as part of your millennial assignment together with your responsibility to rule with Christ (Isaiah 66:18-23).

The world will be organized very differently from how we know it now and all systems will run smoothly. Even the wild animals will have their savage nature transformed so that the lion will lie down in peace with the lamb and eat grass like the cattle (Isaiah 65:25). There will be no harm or destruction whatsoever. That means no plane crashes or car wrecks too.

People in natural bodies who survived the tribulation will continue to have children and that will result in probably the greatest population explosion of all time. They will have natural bodies but will be enabled to live throughout the one thousand years. However, there will still be a handful of cases where natural people who sin will die and not live out the whole one thousand years (Isaiah 65:20). This will be the case because they will still have a choice as to whether they want to be ruled by Jesus or not. Remember, there'll be perhaps billions upon billions of new children born during that time and each will have to make their own choice. However the ultimate test for all those natural people born during the millennial reign will come when Satan is released to test their loyalty as he did with Adam and Eve. Those who follow Satan will go to destruction, whereas those who remain loyal to Christ will be admitted into the New Heavens and the New Earth.

There will be three groups or classes of people in the earth during the millennium. One group will be the glorified saints who came with Jesus from heaven. Another group will be the Jews in natural bodies who will make up the nation of Israel which will be chief among the nations. Then the last group will be composed of the Gentile nations, also in natural bodies, who together with the Jews had survived the tribulation.

The glorified saints who came with Jesus will be the principal rulers or administrators of His kingdom. These will include both Old and New Testament saints who are now in heaven. For example, King David will again be King of the expanded nation of Israel and the twelve apostles of Christ will be Kings under David over each of the twelve tribes of Israel (Ezekiel 37:24-28 and Matthew 19:28). The bible discloses to us that there will be other saints who will be appointed kings over a number of cities which make up nations all over the earth (Luke 19:15-19). You or I could be one of those kings if we faithfully follow the Lord in this life! It is quite evident that some kings or officials of His kingdom will be ranked more highly than others. It all depends on how faithfully they served God in their first life. Listen to me, there will be many other positions of responsibility in the kingdom for those who don't qualify to be kings. There will be need for all kinds of administrators or royal officials to oversee every aspect of the kingdom including agriculture, education, commerce, spiritual ministry, economic development, social affairs, and many other sectors of God's society.

There will be technological advances and milestone achievements in every field of human endeavor. There will be amazing inventions for the betterment of society. We will learn and advance far more than was ever thought possible. It will be a world as no one has ever dreamed. The prosperity that we will know will make what Solomon had, seem like poverty. There will be a perfectly balanced system of wealth distribution. Everyone will have their own property and work to do in the kingdom (Isaiah 65:20-25).

Listen, this is not a fantasy. It is a real world right in front of us and it's coming very soon. The bible tells us that the glorified saints will have special powers including the ability to travel from one geographical location to the other as angels do. They will simply disappear from one location to another as they fulfill their millennial assignments. They will no longer be limited by time and space but like the glorified body of Jesus they will even pass through walls if need be. They will be 'super men' with God-like abilities to know the future, the past and the present supernaturally. They will operate in what the bible calls the powers of the age to come (Hebrews 6:5). That means that the gifts of the Holy Spirit which we know today will operate full-scale in keeping with our glorified state. The glorified saints will be rulers over the natural people and the angels.

I need to also mention that at the inception of the millennial reign, the Lord will miraculously change the climate. This will be a positive climate change unlike what is happening now. There will be a very conducive climate all over the world for agriculture to flourish. It will be so much easier to do farming and other projects. This is because the curse that was pronounced over the land and animals when man fell will be reversed and turned into blessing (Isaiah 25:7-8). The ground will yield increase like we have never known. It will be like having a green house effect all over the planet. The bible also tells us that there will be a new river coming out from under the threshold of the new millennial temple that will flow into the Dead Sea and make its waters fresh so that different kinds of fish will breed abundantly there. There will be a lot of fishing activities along the river and in the formerly Dead Sea. Perhaps by then we will call it the Living Sea or Sea of Life! The river coming from under the millennial temple will bring life wherever it flows. The prophet Ezekiel tells us that *"Fruit trees of all kinds will grow on both banks of the river. Their leaves will not wither, nor will their fruit fail. Every month they will bear, because the water from the sanctuary flows to them. Their fruit will serve for food and their leaves for healing"* (Ezekiel 47:12). That shows us just how blessed and productive nature will be. It will be beautiful and marvelous to be there. I pray you don't miss this and more.

Mind you, this is not the New Jerusalem City that will come from heaven after the millennial reign of Christ. This will be earthly Jerusalem right here on this planet during the millennial reign. It sounds similar to the City above because the earth and earthly Jerusalem will be patterned after Paradise and the heavenly Jerusalem. It has to, since Jesus asked us to pray that the will of God be done on earth as it is in heaven. So that means earth is supposed to look like and operate like heaven now, in the millennial reign and throughout eternity. It is God's desire that the earth be just like heaven.

162

There is no telling what the space programs will be like. But you can rest assured there will be all kinds of projects going – construction of new cities complete with buildings, bridges and other infrastructure never before seen in this world (Isaiah 65:21-23). There will be work to do and all of it with God's unlimited wisdom. We will work, play and praise God.

The whole world will worship God together (Zechariah 14:17). I have no doubt that churches will continue to exist as many tribulation survivors and the children that will be born to them will have to be ministered to by the saints. Yes, we will still preach the gospel and teach the nations throughout the millennial reign. No wonder the Bible calls it the eternal gospel (Revelation 14:6).The work of making disciples will continue (Isaiah 66:18-19). It will be wonderful because in a glorified body you can be preaching in Africa and when you finish you can be translated from there to Asia. That will be the supernatural transportation of the glorified saints. So the makers of *Star Trek* were not too far off when they portrayed their heroes disappearing from one place and appearing in another.

I believe we will be able to explore the outer regions of space in the same way. We will be able to travel at lightening speed and explore the galaxies of our universe that God made for our enjoyment. We will have glorified bodies just like Jesus and so we will be able to travel anywhere supernaturally just like He does. But our greatest pleasure will be to know the Lord more and more and more each day.

I have taken this time to describe the coming world so that you can know that it is real and not some mystical misty world where you just float around on clouds playing harps. No, it will be a time of exercising dominion over all creation as God intended right from the beginning! (Genesis 1:26-28)

The Final Rebellion

"When the thousand years are over, Satan will be released from his prison and go out to deceive the nations in the four corners of the earth – Gog and Magog – to gather them for battle. In number they are like the sand on the seashore. They marched across the breadth of the earth and surrounded the camp of God's people, the city he loves. But fire came down from heaven and devoured them. And the devil, who deceived them, was thrown into the lake of burning sulphur, where the beast and the false prophet had been thrown. They will be tormented day and night for ever and ever." (Revelation 20:7-10)

After the millennial reign is over, Satan will be set free for a short time to tempt those who have been born during the millennium so that they can choose to follow Christ or reject Him. They, like everybody who's lived before, must be given a chance to exercise their free will as far as loyalty to God is concerned. Don't worry. Those who came from heaven with Christ will not in any wise be subject to this temptation. They are forever sealed and are in glorified bodies. It is the tribulation survivors in natural bodies whose many children born during the millennial reign will have to be tested. This will ensure that anybody who is not an infant, who will enter the eternal perfect state after the last judgment, will have made a conscious choice for Jesus instead of Satan. They will have exercised their God-given right to choose their eternal destiny. God will not force anyone to follow Him, but will give each one an opportunity to choose. That's divine justice!

The Great White Throne Judgment

"Just as man is destined to die once, and after that to face judgment" (Hebrews 9: 27).

The story is told of a young man who was involved in a car accident and was rescued from bleeding to death by a compassionate stranger who rushed him to a nearby clinic. After a number of years, the young man committed a serious crime and was in court about to be sentenced. He looked closely at the judge and realized he was the man who had saved him from that fatal accident. With desperation in his voice, he said to the judge, "Your honor, remember me? I'm the boy you rescued from that car accident a few years ago. Please show me mercy, I pray." The judge pointed his finger at him and said, "Young man, yesterday I was your savior, but today I am your judge."

There's a great day of judgment coming and all men must be warned about it. Those who don't accept Jesus as their Savior now will have to face Him as their Judge on that fateful day. *"It is a fearful thing to fall into the hands of the living God"* (Hebrews 10:31). The God of holiness and purity has made a way for everyone to escape that judgment by sending His Son Jesus to bear their punishment for sin so that whoever calls upon His name shall be saved. He does not wish that any one should perish but *"wants all men to be saved and to come to a knowledge of the truth"* (1Timothy 2:4).

"And fear not them which kill the body, but are not able to kill the soul: but rather fear Him which is able to destroy both soul and body in hell" (Matthew 10:28). The God of love is also the God of judgment, and it will do us a lot of good to have this balanced view of Him. He is awesome in judgment and wondrous in love. The Lord Jesus Christ tells us not only to love Him as our Savior, but to also reverence Him as our awesome Judge.

The most dreadful day in all human existence is that great Day of Judgment when all the wicked of all generations will be judged and then thrown into the eternal lake of burning sulfur. It will be all tears and regret for those being judged on that terrible day. This will take place immediately following the millennial reign of Christ and Satan's casting into the lake of fire. The Bible says every knee shall bow and every tongue shall confess that Jesus Christ is Lord to the glory of the Father (Romans 14:10-12). You can either do it voluntarily today or do it by force tomorrow.

The Great White Throne Judgment is also the time when all evil angels will be judged and cast into the Lake of Fire. The saints will judge these angels. Every demon spirit that exists today will be cast into the lake of fire on that day. They will all be tormented day and night forever and ever. But what is even more tragic is that the people who had an opportunity to repent but did not, will also experience eternal punishment with Satan and his cohorts. Jesus makes it clear that this terrible place was never created for man but for the devil and his angels. Yet sadly, many people who follow Satan until they die will have to go there with him. They will burn forever with him. Oh how tragic! The spirits (angels) of death and hell will also be cast into the lake of fire and that is how the last enemy (death) will be destroyed.

The Lord will have resurrected every sinner so that they'll have immortal bodies that will experience eternal fire without being annihilated. They will continue to burn and be tormented throughout the endless ages of eternity. They will experience what the bible calls the second death. It is far more horrific than can be described. So don't choose to go there. Go to heaven instead. Repent and accept Jesus. He's the only hope you have. Don't say you were never told. Find out the truth now and save your precious soul from eternal damnation. You can't afford to wait. Make things right with God now! Accept Jesus while you have the time or else it may be too late.

The New Heavens and the New Earth

Now once the Judgment of the White Throne is over, the Lord will purge the Earth and the heaven or sky surrounding it with fire. This fire will purge the Earth and sky of every impurity and contamination of sin making it fit to be the home of eternal righteousness. This is when the Holy City, New Jerusalem will come down from heaven and be forever united with the new Earth. The heavenly city will become one with the earth and God the Father will now dwell with men in glory forever. This will by far exceed any glory that man has experienced including the Garden of Eden and the millennial reign of Christ. The old order of things will have passed away and a new and eternal order ushered in.

This will be the time we will have all been waiting for – the eternal perfect state that will become more and more glorious throughout the endless ages. The new earth will become a global paradise with lush gardens of splendor, pure rivers, streams and lakes filled with water creatures. The splendor of the earth will by far exceed anything before that time. The conditions will be even more perfect than what was experienced in the millennium. It will be perfection at its highest. The kingdom set-up that existed during the millennial reign will continue in far greater splendor as God the Father Himself will also be present with us.

The New Jerusalem City which will now be one with the new earth will provide great light for all the nations. The bible says, *"The nations will walk by its light, and the kings of the earth will bring their splendor into it"* (Revelation 21:24). The Book of Romans gives us a little more insight into the transition that will take place at the inception of the new heavens and the new earth. *"Then the end will come, when He hands over the kingdom to God the Father after He has destroyed all dominion, authority and power. For He must reign until He has put all His enemies under His feet. The last enemy to be destroyed is death...When He has done this, then the son Himself will be made subject to Him who put everything under Him, so that God may be all in all"* (1 Corinthians 15:24,-26, 28). Now that is the ultimate destiny of mankind!

We are called to a destiny that truly defies description. It is what the bible says no eye has seen, no ear has heard and no mind has conceived (1 Corinthians 2:9). We can only have little glimpses here and there as the Spirit of God permits us. This was what was destined for our glory before time began. The Father will be the Supreme Ruler. Jesus as King of kings and Lord of lords, with His saints will rule over all creation including the angels for the endless ages of eternity. The kingdom that was set up at the beginning of the millennium will continue forever and ever. So if you were a king during the millennium you will continue in that position forever.

Please meditate on the following scriptural passages that speak of how life will be in the eternal perfect state:

"Then the angel showed me the river of the water of life, as clear as crystal, flowing from the throne of God and of the Lamb down the middle of the great street of the city. On each side of the river stood the tree of life, bearing twelve crops of fruit, yielding its fruit every month. And the leaves of the tree are for the healing of the nations. No longer will there be any curse. The throne of God and of the Lamb will be in the city, and His servants will serve Him. They will see His face, and His name will be on their foreheads. There will be no more night. They will not need the light of a lamp or the light of the sun, for the Lord God will give them light. And they will reign forever and ever" (Revelation 22:1-5).

"He who testifies to these things says, "Yes, I am coming soon." Amen. Come, Lord Jesus" (Revelation 22:20).

The Way of Salvation

It is not how many good things you do. It is whether or not you have accepted Jesus Christ as your Lord. You can't do enough good works to earn heaven. You must repent of your self-righteousness and believe on the One who died to save your soul. It would be a crime for me to withhold information that could lead to the salvation of your precious soul. I want to warn you in straight-forward language so that you make up your own mind what you will do about the information.

Trust me, there are people in hell today who thought they still had time to repent. They put off that voice that was telling them, "Turn from your sin and come to Me." They kept changing the TV channel when a preacher came on. They kept saying, "I'm not ready yet," until one day it was too late. If only they could have your opportunity. If only they could have just one moment of repentance. But most unfortunately, that chance is forever gone. See to it that you don't end up like them.

The Bible says, *"Salvation is found in no-one else, for there is no other name under heaven given to men by which we must be saved"* (Acts 4:12). So call on the name of the Lord my friend, for everyone who calls on the name of the Lord shall be saved. *"Repent then and turn to God, so that your sins may be wiped out..."* (Acts 3:19a). Believe in your heart that Jesus Christ shed His blood on the cross to wash your sins away. Accept His sacrifice on your behalf so that He can change you into a brand new person in His image of righteousness and holiness. Through confessing Him as your Lord, you will instantly become a child of the Most High God. The Bible says, *"That if you confess with your mouth, Jesus is Lord, and believe in your heart that God raised Him from the dead, you will be saved"* (Romans 10:9). So if you are serious about missing Hell and making it to Heaven, then pray this prayer out loud from the heart:

"Dear God, I come to You as I am, knowing that You love me with an everlasting love that You demonstrated by sending Jesus to die on the cross for me. I now turn away from my wicked ways and come to you with all my heart. I believe that Jesus is the Son of God Who died and rose again and I accept His sacrifice for my sins. With faith in my heart I now acknowledge Jesus Christ as Lord of my life and purpose to follow Him all the way to heaven. Thank You Father for making me your child today. May your will be done in my life in Jesus' name. Amen."

Congratulations for making that decision and praying that prayer. Your journey into a most glorious future has now begun. Make sure you purchase a Bible if you don't own one and read it daily to feed your new born spirit. The study of God's word will begin to change your thinking so that God's will is revealed to you. I recommend that you first read through the Gospel of John and the Book of Romans to help you understand what it means to be a child of God. Then after this, you can read through the whole New Testament from Matthew to Revelation after which you can read Genesis to Malachi.

The next thing you need to learn is how to pray which is simply talking with God and worshipping Him. Speak to Him as naturally as you would speak with someone in your room but with respect for His greatness. He is your Heavenly Father Who delights to fellowship with His children and take care of their every need.

Thirdly, find a good church that believes in Jesus Christ and the Bible. Ask God to lead you to the right place for you and to give you people who will help you in your new life in Christ. This will be an opportunity to meet other believers who can strengthen you in the faith as you fellowship around God's Word and prayer.

Lastly, tell others about your decision to become a disciple of Christ and tell them how it happened for you. Don't force them to change but do tell them that God loves them and does not want them to end up in hell. Invite them to repent and turn to God so that they too can be forgiven and start a new life in Christ that will take them all the way to Heaven. Ask them if you can lead them in a prayer to receive Jesus Christ as their Lord. If they accept, then go ahead and lead them. If they don't, then you have done your part. Just commit them to God in prayer and ask that He will send another person to speak to them.

Please remember that when you first accept Jesus, that is only the beginning. You now must live your life to fulfill the will of the Father every single day until Jesus comes to take His people to Heaven. You can't do this on your own, but you have to rely on God's grace through the Holy Spirit to enable you to do so.

> *"For the grace of God that brings salvation has appeared to all men. It teaches us to say "No" to ungodliness and worldly passions, and to live self-controlled, upright and godly lives in this present age, while we wait for the blessed hope – the glorious appearing of our great God and Savior, Jesus Christ, who gave Himself for us to redeem us from all wickedness and to purify for Himself a people that are His very own, eager to do what is good"* (Titus 2:11-14).

Accounting for Lost Souls

"Do I take any pleasure in the death of the wicked? Declares the Sovereign Lord. Rather, am I not pleased when they turn from their ways and live?" (Ezekiel 19:23).

God takes no pleasure in the death of the wicked. He does not want anyone to go to hell and suffer the punishment of eternal fire. No one is more hurt when sinners go to hell because no one loves them like He does. He is not willing that any should perish but that all should come to the saving knowledge of His Son, Jesus Christ. He has given believers the task of informing the sinner about His love and the coming judgment so that they can repent and come to Him. He wants every person to hear the message of truth. But if as believers we don't warn the sinner, then the Lord will hold us accountable for our irresponsibility. Every believer surely knows or meets someone they have the opportunity to share the gospel with every so often. It is an awesome responsibility to be entrusted with the eternal salvation of another's soul. Just imagine what would happen if nobody ever told you about Jesus and you stood at the judgment looking at people who knew about this day but never warned you about it. That's just terrible to imagine, isn't it?

We, the Christians, must repent of our indifferent attitude toward the lost. We must ask God to give us a fresh revelation and passion for the lost. We must ask for boldness to go out and preach the gospel to every sinner out there. We must warn the world about the judgment and the fire and brimstone of the lake of fire. We must declare the love and mercy of God to our generation and tell them that if they don't repent they will have to face the most fearsome judgment of all. Like Peter we must plead with them, *"Save yourselves from this corrupt generation"* (Acts 2:40).

This world is in a spiritual state of emergency. Souls are perishing fast and we must rescue as many as we can each day. *"Be merciful to those who doubt; snatch others from the fire and* save them" (Jude 22-23a). That does not mean you will take them from hell itself but that those who are nearly falling in can be rescued even if it's at the last minute.

Friends, Jesus is coming very soon and we must speed up our rescue mission in this world. There are relatives, workmates and friends that still need to be saved. It is the calling of every believer to be salt and light to the world. God will hold us accountable for what we did with the soul winning opportunities He gave us. He promises a soul winner's crown to every faithful soul winner. He also promises that those who lead many to righteousness will shine like the stars forever and ever (Daniel 12:3).

Meditate on this:

> "Son of man, I have made you a watchman for the house of Israel; so hear the word I speak and give them warning from me.
>
> When I say to the wicked, 'O wicked man, you will surely die, and you do not speak out to dissuade him from his ways, that wicked man will die for his sin, and I will hold you accountable for his blood.
>
> But if you do warn the wicked man to turn from his ways and he does not do so, he will die for his sin, but you will have saved yourself" (Ezekiel 33:7-9).

Win Your Own Soul First

> "For what is a man profited, if he shall gain the whole world, and lose his own soul? Or what shall a man give in exchange for his soul? For the Son of man shall come in the glory of His Father with His angels; and then he shall reward every man according to his works" (Matthew 18:26-27).

172

This is one of the most serious statements to ever fall from the lips of the Master. He asks us a couple of questions that we must all pause and think about. The bottom line is: **There is nothing worth losing your soul over.** Your soul is so precious that the whole universe combined can't equal its worth to God. Even for those who are already born again, we are continually warned in scripture about the danger of falling from grace. *"...be on your guard so that you may not be carried away by the error of lawless men and fall from your secure position"* (2 Peter 3:17).

We need to watch over our soul with all diligence. We cannot afford to lose ground or fall from God's grace. We must contend for the faith which was once delivered to the saints and endure to the final end. *"So then, dear friends, since you are looking forward to this, make every effort to be found spotless, blameless and at peace with Him"* (2 Peter 3:14).

Our interaction with the Spirit and Word of God brings forth the character of God that is in our recreated human spirit. *"Christ loved the church and gave Himself up for her to make her holy, cleansing her by the washing of water through the word, and to present her to Himself as a radiant church, without stain or wrinkle or any other blemish, but holy and blameless"* (Ephesians 5:25-27).

The messages to the seven churches in Revelation 2 and 3 give us a picture of how Jesus will judge believers. He starts out by commending them for the good works they've done and then rebukes them for cooling off spiritually. The church at Ephesus was rebuked for losing their first love. They were busy doing things for God but had grown cold in their relationship with Him. So Jesus commanded them to remember the height from which they had fallen and to repent and do the first works or else He would come and remove their lamp-stand from its place. (Revelation 2:4-5). It is very easy for Christians and even preachers to get so busy doing the Lord's work at the expense of spending quality time with the Lord of the work. That is how gradually people lose touch with God and settle into a religious routine. They now get to a place where they have to play "Christian" without having an encounter with God. It is at this stage that some fall into hypocrisy and turn away from God. But this doesn't have to be you, my friend. You can repent and get back to your First Love – Jesus Christ.

Jesus is very serious about our spiritual condition and He will waste no time in rebuking us for our spiritual negligence. Listen to His rebuke to the church at Sardis: "…I know your deeds; you have a reputation of being alive, but you are dead. Wake up! Strengthen what remains and is about to die, for I have not found your deeds complete in the sight of My God" (Revelation 3:1b-2). These are the ones who are empty on the inside but appear as though they are doing fine. They look active but they are no longer abiding in the True Vine that produces life.

The church at Laodicea seems to be even worse. They have all their material needs met but they have gotten to a place where they are neither cold nor hot. They have become lukewarm and Jesus warns that He is about to spit them out of His mouth (Revelation 3:15-16). Their condition is so pathetic because they have one leg in the church and the other leg in the world. The Lord says to them, ***"Those whom I love I rebuke and discipline.*** *So be earnest, and repent"* (Revelation 3:19). It's interesting how Jesus tells the churches to repent and yet many of us think that repentance is just for sinners. True repentance requires a change of heart as well as a change of action.

From these churches we learn that we mustn't take our salvation for granted but treasure and protect it jealously above all things. We must keep our soul pure at all times through ever-increasing fellowship with the Holy Spirit and the Word. Our goal must be to continually abide in Him and His word. That way our spiritual life will be kept at "boiling point" for God. Pray without ceasing. Take some time to fast. Meditate and study God's word day and night and don't neglect fellowship with other believers. Take care of your spiritual life, my friends, and don't give yourself opportunity for backsliding. Aim to have an encounter with Jesus Christ every day. It's not a duty. It's a relationship.

"Watch your life and doctrine closely. Persevere in them, because if you do, you will save both yourself and your hearers" (1 Timothy 4:16). Place your faith in *"Him who is able to keep you from falling and to present you before His glorious presence without fault and with great joy"* (Jude 24). You are not to live in the fear of falling but rather, you are to focus on standing by His grace through your faith.

Jesus is Purifying His Church

> *"Blessed are the pure in heart, for they shall see God"* (Matthew 5:8).

A pure heart is a heart that is established in righteousness. The purity of Christ in your spirit must translate into purity of mind so that your thoughts and motives will produce pure deeds that will glorify God. A holy life is the by-product of abiding in the Holy One and letting His holy word abide in us. It is our responsibility to cooperate with the Spirit of Holiness to produce the life of holiness that God so desires. *"For God did not call us to be impure, but to live a holy life"* (1 Thessalonians 4:7). The will of God is the total sanctification of our spirit, soul and body. He wants us to resemble Christ in purity and holiness for we are called to be like Him. A holy life is not lived by keeping a set of rules but by abiding in the Holy One thus allowing His holy nature to be expressed through us. Holy living is a natural consequence of being intimate with the Holy Spirit.

God wants to purify the church for His coming and will purify those who yield to His Spirit. *"He will sit as a refiner and purifier of silver; he will purify the Levites and refine them like gold and silver. Then the Lord will have men who will bring offerings in righteousness"* (Malachi 3:3). This is what God is doing in the church until the ready spiritual virgins whose lamps are burning brightly are taken to the marriage feast in heaven.

Purity is a very big word with many shades of meaning. I consulted Webster's Universal English Dictionary to help us see its expanded meaning. To be pure means to be clean, spotless, stainless, unadulterated, unalloyed, unblemished, uncorrupted, undefiled, unpolluted, untainted, untarnished, innocent, virgin, virtuous, genuine, and perfect. This is a description of the end time church that Jesus Christ wants to come and find. It must be a church that is pure in thought, word and deed. This is the victorious church of the last days. Will you be a part of it? This purity is already in our spirit man but needs to translate into pure living.

One of the agencies Jesus uses to purify the church is His holy and precious Word. This word will purify our minds so that we can think and act holy in keeping with the purity of Christ in us. The Psalmist of old also believed that the word was instrumental in helping him live a pure life as is said in Psalm 119:9, 11: *"How can a young man keep his way pure? By living according to your word...I have hidden your word in my heart that I might not sin against you."* God's word in our hearts will govern our thinking which will influence our actions. This ties up very well with Romans 12:2 where we are told to be transformed by the renewing of our minds. The mind plays a vital role in determining our behavior. If our mind is carnal we will make carnal decisions. But if our mind is renewed with God's word we will make right choices. *"For to be carnally minded is death; but to be spiritually minded is life and peace"* (Romans 8:6). Like I mentioned earlier, we must rely on His grace to teach *"us to say 'No' to ungodliness and worldly passions, and to live self-controlled, upright and godly lives in this present age, while we wait for the blessed hope – the glorious appearing of our great God and Savior, Jesus Christ"* (Titus 2:12-13).

CHAPTER 8

WARNING TO THE WORLD

I must warn everyone who I possibly can that every chance that they have to repent could be their very last. I am warning everyone reading this book to think seriously about their life in relation to the limited time we have left on this planet to repent. We must take warning from Noah's example who heeded God's warning and warned the people of his generation about the impending judgment that was about to fall. *"By faith Noah, when warned about things not yet seen, in holy fear built an ark to save his family. By his faith he condemned the world and became heir of the righteousness that comes by faith"* (Hebrews 11:7). The bible actually calls Noah a preacher of righteousness meaning that he preached to the people of his generation the messages that God gave him (2 Peter 2:5).

Warning #1   Get Ready or Remain

Jesus, in explaining the prevailing conditions on earth before His return, uses Noah's time as an example.

> *"No one knows about that day or hour, not even the angels in heaven, nor the Son, but only the Father. As it was in the days of Noah, so it will be at the coming of the Son of Man. For in the days before the flood, people were eating and drinking, marrying and giving in marriage, up to the day Noah entered the ark; and they knew nothing about what would happen until the flood came and took them all away. That is how it will be at the coming of the Son of man...So you also must be ready, because the Son of Man will come at an hour when you do not expect him"* (Matthew 24:36-39, 44)

Because we do not know when Jesus is coming, we must be ready at all times. We must live rapture-ready because the trumpet could blow at any moment. I am sure you do not want to face the disappointment of being left behind after the trumpet has blown.

Some may wonder what trumpet I'm referring to. Well the Apostle Paul puts it very clearly in 1 Thessalonians 4:15:

> *"According to the Lord's own word, we tell you that we who are still alive, who are left till the coming of the Lord, will certainly not precede those who have fallen asleep. For the Lord himself will come down from heaven, with a loud command, with the voice of the archangel and with the trumpet call of God, and the dead in Christ will rise first. After that, we who are still alive and are left will be caught up together with them in the clouds to meet the Lord in the air. And so we will be with the Lord forever."*

This, event popularly known as the rapture, is our transportation to heaven. Yet we all know that even though you may have an air ticket you can still miss your flight if you are not ready and waiting at the airport. If you are scheduled to fly at 10:00hrs and you arrive at the airport at 10:15hrs hoping that somehow the plane would be waiting for you, then you've got something else coming! The transport should not be waiting for the passenger, but rather the passenger for the transport! So by the same token, we also must be constantly ready especially that our transport could show up and take off at any moment.

WARNING #2   An Alliance of Nations Will Attack Israel (Ezekiel 38 and 39)

Either before or right after the rapture, an alliance of nations, some of whom have been specifically named like Persia (an ancient name for Iran) and Cush (an ancient name for Sudan), will unite against Israel in pretty much the same way the world united against Iraq's invasion of Kuwait. It is fairly clear from the prophetic writings of Ezekiel that this alliance of nations will predominantly be made up of Islamic Arab nations who have been at loggerheads with Israel for a very long time now.

Many bible scholars have concluded that the identity of the leading nation in this alliance is present-day Russia. From my examination of that passage it is very likely that these scholars are correct. It says, *"Son of man, prophesy against Gog and say: This is what the Sovereign Lord says: I am against you O Gog, chief prince of Meshech and Tubal. I will turn you around and drag you along. I will bring you from the far north and send you against the mountains of Israel"* (Ezekiel 39:1-2). This leading nation from the far north of Israel can easily be pin-pointed by anyone who has a world map or atlas. If you took a pencil or a ruler and you placed it vertically with one end on Israel and followed it up to the far north, what nation do you find? You will find Russia!

I don't suppose that's a prophetic mystery for anybody. It's just that simple. Haven't you ever wondered why Russia and Iran get along so well? Russia has actually been helping Iran become a military power for decades now. It is interesting to note that a huge percentage of the Russian army is Moslem. So an alliance with Islamic countries is not only possible but almost inevitable. What you need to understand is that Russia has always wanted to regain its superpower status ever since the demise of the Soviet Union. They want the status they used to have.

But what is so amazing about this event is how that God intervenes right in the middle of the whole attack and puts it to an abrupt end supernaturally. The scenario is painted as follows (I hope you can see all the news cameras covering this event):

> *"This is what will happen in that day: When Gog attacks the land of Israel, my hot anger will be aroused, declares the Sovereign Lord. In my zeal and fiery wrath I declare that at that time there shall be a great earthquake in the land of Israel. The fish of the sea, the birds of the air, the beasts of the field, every creature that moves along the ground, and all the people on the face of the earth will*

tremble at my presence. The mountains will be overturned, the cliffs will crumble and every wall will fall to the ground. I will summon a sword against Gog on all my mountains, declares the Sovereign Lord. Every man's sword will be against his brother. I will execute judgment upon him with plague and bloodshed; I will pour down torrents of rain, hailstones and burning sulphur on him and on his troops and on the many nations with him. And so I will show my greatness and my holiness, and I will make myself known in the sight of many nations. Then they will know that I am the Lord." (Ezekiel 38:18-23).

This remarkable event is something the world needs to take warning for because it's very close. This event is not the battle of Armageddon at the appearing of Christ and His heavenly armies. At Armageddon the nation of Israel will fight (Zechariah 14:14), but in this event no mention is made of Israel's defense except that the Lord intervenes to show His glory.

WARNING #3   The Antichrist Is A Deceiver

At the time of this writing, I am more convinced than ever that the stage for the Antichrist is set. The world is fast moving towards a one world government, economy and religious system. The political, economic, social and religious crises rocking the world are paving the way for a one world system with more control measures over each nation. The mark of the beast economic system has reached an advanced stage. A lot of the regional economic groupings in the world are just paving the way for the Antichrist's system of commerce where no one will be allowed to buy or sell anything unless they have the mark which is actually the name of the Beast or the number of his name on their right hand or their forehead. There is no redemption for those who receive this mark. They are doomed forever. Those who refuse to receive the mark or worship the Beast will have to be executed. Yet it is far better to believe in Christ and be executed for refusing to commit idolatry than to seal your own eternal doom. These things will take place during the seven year tribulation after the ready saints have been taken to heaven.

The Antichrist's rise to power is not through war and bloodshed as you may suppose. He will rise to power through diplomacy. He will deceive the world through his peace agenda whose ultimate aim is world conquest. He will endeavor to establish himself as the centre of world worship. This was and still is Satan's agenda. He wants the worship that belongs only to God. Remember, he even offered Jesus the kingdoms of this world if only He would bow down and worship him. There will be many who will be deceived into worshipping both the dragon (Satan) and the Beast (the Antichrist). *"Men worshipped the dragon because he had given authority to the beast, and they also worshipped the Beast and asked, "Who is like the beast? Who can make war against him?"* (Revelation 13:4). So do take warning: the Antichrist is coming. Better to be prepared and go in the rapture than to face him. Now, if you are reading this book after the rapture has already taken place, then know that it is better to be killed for believing in Jesus and go to heaven than to fear death and bow down to the Beast and be eternally lost.

WARNING #4   The Tribulation Will Be Most Terrible

The tribulation is a seven year period beginning at the time of the rapture and ending with the battle of Armageddon at the return of Christ with His saints. The antichrist will have entered into a seven year peace treaty with Israel and for the first three and a half years there will be some peace. But he will violate that agreement and set in motion the last three and a half years of great tribulation.

> *"For then there will be great distress, unequaled from the beginning of the world until now – and never to be equaled again. If those days had not been cut short, no one would survive, but for the sake of the elect those days will be shortened"* (Matthew 24:21-22).

The tribulation is not the time you would want to be alive on this earth. You must make things right with God now so that you can escape this time of wrath. There will be so much death that at one point a third of the world's population then will have died. The book of Revelation records that: *"A third of mankind was killed by the three plagues of fire, smoke and sulfur"* (Revelation 9:18). That's a holocaust if you ever saw one. It will make all our world wars, holocausts and genocides seem small by comparison. Now, supposing there were 6 billion people on earth during the tribulation, it means 2 billion of those would be killed by the three plagues. That's not counting those who will be killed by the Antichrist and other causes. No wonder Jesus said that those days will have to be cut short or else no life will remain.

WARNING # 5   Armageddon Is Coming

The bloodiest battle to ever take place will be at the conclusion of the tribulation period when Jesus and His heavenly armies return to takeover planet earth. The day on which this battle takes place is known as "the great day of God Almighty" (Revelation 16:14). That battle is known as the Battle of Armageddon. That is the day the Lord will reveal Himself as a Mighty Man of War Who alone is the "Unconquerable Warrior."

The Antichrist will attempt to fight this seemingly 'alien invasion' of planet earth. He will be backed by the largest and most well equipped earthly army ever assembled. He will have already captured the earthly city of Jerusalem when Jesus and His saints appear on earth (Zechariah 14:2-4). The Antichrist will seem totally invincible until the real Christ shows up. Remember, if you had gone to heaven in the rapture seven years earlier or you died in Christ before this time, you will be one of the riders on white horses coming to invade this planet with Jesus.

I have chosen some verses from Matthew 24 and Revelation 19 to describe what will happen when Jesus Christ and His armies are revealed. Take a look at this:

> *"Immediately after the distress of those days the sun will be darkened, and the moon will not give its light; the stars will fall from the sky, and the heavenly bodies will be*

shaken. At that time the sign of the Son of Man will appear in the sky, and all the nations of the earth will mourn. They will see the Son of Man coming on the clouds of the sky, with power and great glory" (Matthew 24:29-30).

"I saw heaven standing open and there before me was a white horse, whose rider is called Faithful and True. With justice he judges and makes war.

The armies of heaven were following him, riding on white horses and dressed in fine linen, white and clean.

Then I saw the beast and the kings of the earth and their armies gathered together to make war against the rider on the horse and his army" (Revelation 19:11, 14, 19).

Now let's pause here a moment before we continue this great scenario. The panorama of glory that will be displayed is unlike anything ever witnessed since creation. The immense light of Christ, together with that of His glorified saints and angels, will be far brighter that a million suns shining at the same time. There will be no doubt as to whether this is Jesus or not. Every Earth dweller will be able to see this most glorious of events. The bible says that every eye shall see Him. The Pygmies in the jungles of Africa, the Aboriginals in Australia, the Eskimos in the north pole, the isolated tribes living in the Amazon and every city, town and village dweller, not to mention the Islanders will see the Son of Man coming from heaven with power and exceedingly great glory. **Can you see the billions of angels with wings spread and the Lord and His innumerable saints descending to the earth in heavenly glory?**

Now let's pick up our story where we left off. *"But the Beast was captured, and with him the False Prophet who had performed the miraculous signs on his behalf. With these signs he had deluded those who had received the mark of the beast and worshipped his image. The two of them were thrown alive into the fiery lake of burning sulfur. The rest of them were killed with the sword that came out of the mouth of the rider on the horse, and all the birds gorged themselves on their flesh"* (Revelation 19:20-21). The number of dead bodies in this conflict is undoubtedly more than in any other conflict since the day Cain killed Abel. The army from the East alone which will number 200 million will perish at this point creating a river of blood where the river Euphrates once flowed. The other armies from the north, south and west will be among those that will be slain by the sword of the Lord so that the number of casualties will be enormous indeed. It will also take an army of vultures and other birds of prey to help clean up this mess of human bodies on the ground.

Please take some time to read the whole of chapter 14 of the book of Zechariah to get more details of what happens during this cataclysmic conflict.

Brace Yourself for Change

Many of us have no idea what is about to transpire on this planet. But if we get to know about it, we can prepare and not be caught by surprise. My spiritual mentor used to say, "To be forewarned is to be forearmed," which in this case means that those who are armed with knowledge of the future can best prepare for it.

The book you hold in your hands is a roadmap to the future of planet Earth and its inhabitants. It will help you know what to do before the future arrives. So brace yourself for change, for it is surely coming!

The world we live in is about to go through the most radical if not cataclysmic changes any generation has ever seen or ever will see. Why? It's because we're in the grand finale. We are finishing off what started after Jesus died and rose again. We are the end-time people. We are living in the most exciting generation that anyone could ever hope to live in because ours is the generation that has seen more prophetic fulfillment than any other. We might just be the generation that will usher in the glorious return of our Lord for His radiant church. "Be very careful, then, how you live – not as unwise but as wise, making the most of every opportunity, because the days are evil" (Ephesians 5:15-16). **Jesus Christ is coming back very soon, and it may be sooner than you think.** "*You also must be ready, because the Son of Man will come at an hour when you do not expect him*" (Luke 12:40). We are the most enlightened generation and we will have to account for more.

Tribulation Survival
(A Message to Those Left Behind)

If you are reading this book after a mass disappearance of people from the earth, then you have missed the coming of Jesus to take away the ready saints to heaven. It means that you are now in the seven year tribulation period before Jesus returns with the saints to set up His 1000 year rule on the earth.

"Suddenly Millions Disappear!" "Why have people gone missing?" Perhaps these and many more will be the news headlines right after the rapture. This mysterious disappearance of people from the earth is not the work of aliens or terrorists. It is a fulfillment of Jesus' promise to take His prepared people to heaven so that they do not have to go through this seven year period of great trouble in the earth.

The world should definitely be in a state of chaos politically, economically and socially. The fear and anxiety that many are experiencing will lead them to seek able leadership to show them the way. They will need someone to give them hope in this state of confusion. That someone, the bible says, is the Antichrist who will first appear as a man of peace with a message of hope for a confused world. He, together with a group of world leaders will set up a one world government which will introduce a one world economic, social and religious system. He will come under the guise of bringing hope and restoration to the world. He will sign a peace treaty with Israel and will restructure the way things are run in this world.

He will seek to kill anyone who doesn't receive his mark on their hand or forehead. The False Prophet will also back this world leader with some of the most spectacular signs, wonders and mighty miracles that are of satanic origin. This False Prophet will erect an idol that resembles this world leader. This is when worldwide idol, satanic and Antichrist worship will officially be instituted. Men and women will be forced to worship the image of this world leader, failure to which they will be killed. No one will be allowed to buy or sell unless they first receive the mark of the Beast which is his name or the number of his name. Those who worship the Beast and receive his mark will have sealed their own eternal doom. There's only eternal fire left for them.

So the only hope for those of you that are left behind is to commit your life to the true Messiah, Jesus Christ, by calling upon His name. He is the only one who died on the cross to save you from your sins. He is the only hope you have of spending eternity with God. You must believe in your heart that God raised Him from the dead and that He and only He is the true Savior of the world. Pray this prayer out loud to receive Jesus as your Lord.

Heavenly Father I come to you as I am. I accept the sacrifice of Jesus Christ on the cross for me. I now confess Jesus as my Lord and determine to follow Him even to the point of death. I believe I am now a child of God washed in the blood of Jesus. I have been made a new creation in Christ. Thank you, Father, for saving me. Now help me live my life for your glory. Amen.

Now that you've made Jesus the Lord of your life, here are some crucial steps for you to follow during the tribulation:

1. **Do not by any means or in any way accept the mark or number of the beast on your forehead, hand or any other part of your body for that matter.** Don't have anything to do with it. They will not allow you to buy or sell without the mark, meaning that many people will get

the mark for their own economic survival. But you, my friend, don't have to. You must do all you can in the natural and trust God to provide for your needs. He provided food and drink for the Israelites in the wilderness and He can certainly provide for you. Read Psalm 23 and make it your prayer.

2. **Do not at any time bow down in worship to this world leader called the Beast or the image that the False Prophet sets up.** People will be forced to worship the beast and his image but like Shadrach, Meshach and Abednego refused to bow to King Nebuchadnezzar's idolatrous image, refuse to bow down. Read Daniel chapter 3. If it means losing your life for the sake of Christ, let them kill you. You will have been a martyr for Jesus. If they kill you, your spirit goes to be with Jesus in heaven where you will receive the crown of life. Please take the time to read the entire book of Revelation. It will help you understand what is happening and give you hope in the midst of chaos.

3. **Get a copy of the bible and read it daily, starting with the gospel of John, and then the book of Romans.** After this you can read the book of Daniel and Revelation. When you are through, read the entire Bible starting with the New Testament and then the Old. Follow God's word and you will not be deceived by the Antichrist and the False Prophet. Hold on to God's word for dear life, and put into practice everything you learn.

4. **Pray to God daily in the name of Jesus Christ.** The Father will hear you and answer you during this time of great trouble. Take the time to pray Psalm 91 and expect God to fulfill His Word. It is possible to survive the tribulation, unless you willingly lay down your life as a martyr for Jesus. Either way, you win! But in the meantime, be faithful in prayer every day that you live. Pray the prayers that Paul prayed for the Ephesian church in Ephesians 1:16-21 and 3:14-21. Team up with other believers and pray together for God's will to be done in your lives and in the world at large. Pray for all

the saints and sinners as well. I need not remind you that you need to lead as many people to Jesus as possible until His return to take over the earth.

CONCLUSION - OUR GLORIOUS FUTURE

A most glorious future awaits every believer in Christ Jesus. We are destined for glory and ought to demonstrate more and more of it as we see the day approaching. I believe the process of glorification began when we accepted Jesus Christ as our Lord. This process will continue until Jesus comes to find a glorious church without spot or wrinkle. That is the church He will take to heaven.

"But in keeping with His promise we are looking forward to a new heaven and a new earth, the home of righteousness" (2 Peter 3:13). God has revealed just enough about that new world to make us want to be a part of it. In fact, a very short while from now, the trumpet call of God will sound and the dead in Christ shall rise and then those of us who are alive and spiritually ready shall be caught up together with them in the clouds to meet the Lord in the air.

This will signal the beginning of a new order for us as we head for the Judgment Seat of Christ to give an account for our lives and to be rewarded accordingly. We will be receiving our eternal responsibilities in heaven while the earth undergoes a seven year tribulation period. We will then be presented before God the Father on what we would call 'Presentation Day' after which the Marriage Supper of the Lamb can begin. It will be the most spectacular marriage ceremony of all time, and oh, you don't want to miss it! It will be the joining together of the eternal Bridegroom and His eternal Bride in the holiest of matrimonies to ever be conducted. The resplendent glory of it is beyond words. It's the ultimate love story where we'll truly live happily ever after! *"Let us rejoice and be glad and give him glory! For the wedding of the Lamb has come, and his bride has made herself ready"* (Revelation 19:7). Now, for anyone who has ever doubted that the bride of Christ is the eternal Church of God, there's your scripture right there! It includes both New Testament believers and Old Testament ones as well. It is composed of every righteous person who has ever lived.

The next verse even tells us what our wedding dress will look like: "Fine linen, bright and clean, was given her to wear. [Fine linen stands for the righteous acts of the saints]." (Revelation 19:8) You are called to be a part of that bride. Will you accept the proposal? Are you willing to receive the "engagement ring" of salvation today so that when the wedding day comes you will be clad in that glorious attire?

But that is only the beginning. There is so much more ahead of this newly married couple. The Father has provided all that is needed for the most glorious future imaginable. Oh what a life it will be! So after the wedding supper, the Bridegroom and His lovely bride will mount their white horses and ride majestically out of heaven to overwhelmingly defeat the antichrist and His armies who will have gathered together to fight against the King of kings. This most famous of battles is known as the battle of Armageddon at which the Lord Jesus Christ and His armies will emerge totally victorious. The antichrist and the false prophet will be cast alive into the eternal lake of fire.

The next thing on the agenda will be to conduct the Judgment of Israel and the Judgment of the Nations in order to qualify those who get to be a part of the millennial kingdom. This is where the parable of the sheep and goats comes in. The bible reveals that the goats will be sent to eternal fire while the sheep will enter the kingdom prepared for them by the Father from the foundation of the world. Then will begin the thousand-year reign of Christ with His saints. There will be peace, righteousness and prosperity as the rule of Christ is enforced all over this planet.

Then at the end of that glorious millennial reign, the devil and his angels who were imprisoned at the start of the millennium will be released for a season to tempt those who had never been tempted before. Those who came with Jesus from heaven and the martyrs who were resurrected at His coming will not be subjected to this final temptation. They are glorified saints and are not subject to temptation. It is the natural people who survived the great tribulation and continued to have children during the millennium, whose children must choose whether to rebel or remain faithful to the Lord Jesus Christ. One thing is certain: there will be no one in heaven or the new earth that was forced to be there. God wants everyone to voluntarily follow Him. They must choose their own destiny.

Those who choose to follow Satan will gang up in an attempt to overthrow the righteous government of Christ. They will surround the camp of God's people but all of a sudden fire will come down from heaven and devour them. Then comes my favorite part where the archenemy of God and man, Satan, will finally be thrown into the lake of burning sulfur. He will join the antichrist and the false prophet who will have been burning for one thousand years. They will experience the worst of torments forever and ever.

The last event before the new heavens and the new earth will be the Great White Throne Judgment where the ungodly of every generation since Adam's time will be judged. This most fearsome of all judgments, will forever seal the doom of every wicked man. The saddest thing about it is that every single one of these human beings could have repented while on earth but did not. How sad it will be, not just for them, but for God! I cannot imagine the pain in God's heart.

Don't take a chance to go there. The bible says, *"And I saw the dead, great and small, standing before the throne, and books were opened. Another book was opened, which is the book of life. The dead were judged according to what they had done as recorded in the books...If anyone's name was not found written in the book of life, he was thrown into the lake of fire"* (Revelation 20:12 and 15). Everyone that has rejected Jesus as Lord will join the devil, his angels, the antichrist and false prophet in being tormented day and night forever and ever. They will not cease to exist as some suggest. They will forever experience the worst imaginable grief and pain.

The Eternal Perfect State

Now, after Satan, the fallen angels, and all wicked men are banished from God's presence, God can then create a new heaven and a new earth, the eternal home of righteousness. The New Jerusalem City will be merged with the New Earth to form a perfect unity of heaven and earth. The wonder and splendor of this eternal home is simply beyond words. The spirit world and the natural will work in perfect harmony as God originally intended.

The New Earth will by far exceed the old earth in splendor and beauty as much as the glorified saint in Christ exceeds the fallen man. The earth itself will have become "born again" and undergone a "baptism of fire" for purification. The Lord God Jehovah will then turn the purified earth into a global paradise that will endure forever and ever. What will make it even more interesting is that this new earth will have more land area than the old. The earth today is covered with 71% water and only 29% land, while the new earth will have no ocean or sea but will instead have beautiful rivers, streams, lakes and ponds. I can imagine beautiful waterfalls, mountain ranges, wild life, and perhaps even prehistoric animals like dinosaurs, together with angels and people living in perfect harmony. God's purpose for creation will have at last been fully achieved where all creatures in heaven and earth give Him 100% glory. Those who will make it there will enjoy the most blissful life imaginable.

The overcomers will shine far more brightly than the angels. They will actually rule over angels in glorious majesty. It will be the most meaningful life that can possibly be lived and men will finally be allowed to see God the Father's face that Moses longed to see. We will serve God, worship God, fellowship with one another, interact with the angels, eat of the fruit of the tree of life, drink of the water of life freely, and learn more and more about God's creation and His purposes.

Can you see yourself there? Can you see yourself dressed in a royal white robe with a golden crown on your head? Can you picture yourself taking a ride on your white horse to visit a galaxy somewhere? Are you able to see yourself in heavenly glory sitting on a throne and giving angels tasks to accomplish? Are you able to see yourself in a glorified body that shines brightly like the sun? Well, that's the glory that awaits you in the next life.

> *"And I heard a loud voice from the throne saying, 'Now the dwelling of God is with men, and He will live with them. They will be His people, and God Himself will be with them and be their God.'*
>
> *He who overcomes will inherit all this, and I will be his God and he will be my son.*
>
> *There will be no more night. They will not need the light of a lamp or the light of the sun, for the Lord God will give them light. And they will reign forever and ever.*
>
> *He who testifies to these things says, Yes, I am coming soon. Amen. Come, Lord Jesus"*

(Revelation 21:3, 7; 22:5, 20).

I hope this book has and will continue to be a blessing to you. May you run your race and finish your course with joy.

I wish to conclude this book by repeating a key verse that best summarizes the message contained herein:

> *"For we must all appear and be revealed as we are before the Judgment Seat of Christ, so that each may receive [his pay] according to what he has done in the body, whether good or evil [considering what his purpose and motive have been, and what he has achieved, been busy with, and given himself and his attention to accomplishing]"*

(1 Corinthians 5:10 AMP).

To contact the author:

Email: <u>simms.mulozi@gmail.com</u>

Write: Simms Mulozi
       c/o Spirit Generation Media
       1154 Morningside Ave
       Schenectady, NY 12309

About the Author

Simms S. Mulozi communicates with an enthusiasm that captures the heart, stimulates the mind and inspires action. Simms was born and raised in Lusaka, Zambia where he makes his home. Simms involves himself in many endeavors as a minister, educator, businessman, and singer.

www.ingramcontent.com/pod-product-compliance
Lightning Source LLC
LaVergne TN
LVHW011229080426
835509LV00005B/399